More praise for *Jesus Wept*

"In plain and powerful images, Barbara Crafton uses her own journey through clinical depression to shine helpful light on this common and yet rarely understood human condition. She cuts through the usual evasions and reveals interior dialogues that will encourage both sufferers and those who love them."

—Tom Ehrich, president,
Morning Walk Media Inc., and author,
Church Wellness; *Just Wondering, Jesus*;
and *With Scripture as My Compass*

JESUS WEPT

WHEN FAITH AND DEPRESSION MEET

Barbara Cawthorne Crafton

JOSSEY-BASS
A Wiley Imprint
www.josseybass.com

Published by Jossey-Bass
A Wiley Imprint
989 Market Street, San Francisco, CA 94103-1741—www.josseybass.com

Jossey-Bass books and products are available through most bookstores. To contact Jossey-Bass directly call our Customer Care Department within the U.S. at 800-956-7739, outside the U.S. at 317-572-3986, or fax 317-572-4002.

Jossey-Bass also publishes its books in a variety of electronic formats. Some content that appears in print may not be available in electronic books.

Library of Congress Cataloging-in-Publication Data

Crafton, Barbara Cawthorne.
    Jesus wept : when faith and depression meet / Barbara Cawthorne Crafton. — 1st ed.
      p. cm.
    Includes bibliographical references (p.   ).
    ISBN 978-0-470-37195-4 (cloth)
    1. Depression, Mental—Religious aspects—Christianity.   2. Depressed persons—Religious life. I. Title.
    BV4910.34.C73   2009
    248.8'625—dc22
                                                  2008055676

Printed in the United States of America
FIRST EDITION
HB Printing 10 9 8 7 6 5 4 3 2 1

The Geranium Farm is a worldwide community,
numbering in the tens of thousands and dedicated to
the encouragement of spiritual growth. We connect with
one another primarily through the Internet. Many
Farmers responded with great generosity and candor to
my request for their stories of life in the shadow of
clinical depression. Some of their words are used here,
with their permission. To protect their privacy,
their names have all been changed. But they
know who they are.
This book could not have been written without
their help, and so it is dedicated to them, with
much gratitude.

CONTENTS

PREFACE   ix

PROLOGUE. WHAT WE'RE TALKING ABOUT   xiii

1

Jesus Wept   1

2

A Learning Experience   13

WORRY   23

3

I Just Don't Feel Anything   25

4

Trouble in Paradise   37

THE MAGIC KINGDOM   47

5

Charged with the Care of Souls   49

AARON   55

6

The Defendant as Prosecutor   57

7

This Is My Last Hope   73
ELECTRIC POEM   85

8

Sorrowful Mysteries   87

9

The Dark Night   101
INFERNO, CANTO I   109

10

Words Fail Me   111

11

Wanting to Die   129
TO BE OR NOT TO BE   141

12

The Family Disease   143

NOTES   157

FURTHER READING   161

THE AUTHOR   163

PREFACE

There were dire warnings of dreadful heat and humidity for today; it would be hot enough to wilt the briskest of spirits. But it's turned out to be not that bad here. We haven't even needed to turn on the fan upstairs. Sometimes the terrible things a person expects to happen just don't. You gear up for the worst, and then an anticlimactic little inconvenience is all you get. It's almost a disappointment; now where am I going to put all that worry?

Somewhere far away, I hope. Worry beforehand has so little of any use to contribute to what actually happens—it neither causes nor cures anything, ever. I do not think it prepares us for misfortunes in any good way—it simply gives us the chance to experience every sorrow twice, once before it happens and then again when it does. I, for one, would rather be strolling down the sidewalk without a care in the world one day and be crushed by a falling grand piano, than creep fearfully around every corner, afraid that something bad is lurking on the other side.

Well, but if you had known about the baby grand, you wouldn't have walked down that street. You would have taken a different route. Maybe, maybe not. They fall fast, those baby grands. By the time I had enough information about the impending disaster to choose another route, the piano would already be on the ground, with me flat as a cartoon beneath it.

Of course, such sensible reasons not to worry are only effective for people who already don't. Those for whom anxiety is a regular visitor can't turn it off easily in response to reasonable and convincing argument. Chronic fear is not about lack of information: it comes from within. The same is true of chronic sorrow: it does no good to point out to the sufferer that she is really blessed in many ways, that things really aren't so bad, that many other people have it much worse, even if all those things are true. Depression comes from within, not from outside us.

There can be so many reasons for these internal woes. The brain's chemistry authors many of them, and they improve markedly with the right medicine, rightly managed. The trauma of early life or current stress often contributes to this sorry chemical soup, and often the right talk therapy or behavioral therapy helps. Many people spend years struggling to understand themselves and to heal.

For many years, I've thought about how religious faith helps or hinders this struggle, which is my own and that of many other people. Just how prayer might be a means toward healing, and how difficult it can be for those afflicted in this way to pray at all. How hard it can be to heed and act on Jesus' words, *Let not your heart be troubled*, without either lying or sounding falsely pious. Whether you're religious or not, one thing is certain: depression is not for sissies. Living with it is hard.

PROLOGUE: WHAT WE'RE TALKING ABOUT

Everybody gets sad now and then. You're sad when your mother dies; you cry every day, maybe several times a day, perhaps for weeks or even months. Or you're sad when you lose your job. You move away from the old neighborhood, and you're sad to leave all those dear people.

Sorrow comes and then, after a time, it goes. Almost always, it leaves a scar—a big one or a little one, depending on what it is. But sorrow is the usual human response to loss. Sorrow is as normal as toenails. And it's not what this book is about.

Depression *isn't* something everybody has. It is not normal. While it may take root in the shock of a sudden sorrow or a profound life change, it may also just come for no reason at all that the naked eye can see, invited in by a wrong-place-at-the-wrong-time neurochemical moment which is hidden from public view. Depression is the sapping of spiritual strength and joy, the graying of everything. Its onset can be sudden—or it can be gradual, a growing awareness that something is missing and nothing is working as it should, a creeping inability to honor any of one's own achievements or claim any of one's own blessings.

> Depression for me is the ever-present cloud that sits most of the time just to the side of my vision, not so much menacing as simply present, constant witness to its presence and capacity to reenter my life with no more notice than an ordinary Sunday afternoon.
>
> —MARTY

Among many other things, depression is a profound mistrust of the self: it anxiously asks the world for validation, but then can never seem to hear anything back but negative criticism. It leaps to bitter conclusions: *This is my fault. This won't work. I can't do anything right. Things never work out well for me.* And it distrusts whatever positive feedback the world offers in rebuttal: *What do they know?* depression asks scornfully. *If people really knew me, they'd be singing a different tune.*

> I feel shaky when I think about my depression. It can resurface in an instant.
>
> —PATRICIA

And depression confounds those who must live alongside it. They offer what counsel they have, the things that have worked well in *their* lives to ease them out of sorrow, not realizing that depression and sorrow are not the same thing: *Think pleasant thoughts. Spend time in nature. Cuddle your cat. Always remember that the glass is half full, not half empty. Think of all the things you do so well. Remember that God loves you. Remember that I love you.* You listen patiently and feel more alone than ever: the one you love most does not understand you. Alone, and furious with yourself, because— once in a while—you know that it is not the one who loves you who does not understand: it is you. It is you who no longer understand the world. You know that the positive things he is saying are absolutely true, that she is right about all these things, that they would all help if you could just do them. You may know this, in your mind—but your spirit does *not* know. You are hopelessly out of step with the parade of life, and you cannot seem to find your way back into it on your own. This insight fills you with shame. It's not enough that you have been robbed of all your joy: you must also confront the fact that it was an inside job. *I am doing this to myself.*

Sometimes you are not even sure you *want* to find your way back.

> Another attribute of the misery associated with chronic fear and chronic sorrow is that, perversely, I like them, and do not really want to let them go. They confirm me.
>
> —FRANKLIN

Yes, you think, *life may very well be beautiful. But I can't live it. It is just too heavy.* Sometimes you just want to lie very still and let the hours pass. Let weeks pass, years, whatever, as long as you can be still. The level of your exhaustion appalls you.

> When I can pull myself out of the well-worn groove of thoughts of lack: not enough money, not enough talent, not enough intelligence, not enough support, not enough . . . whatever, and when I can list my many blessings, light edges the clouds. . . . The odd thing to me is realizing I can make this choice, but refusing to do so.
>
> —MARIE

Of course, not all depression is that profound. Many people have a habit of life that enshrines it without really knowing that's what it is: a dreary template of mild discouragement into which everything must somehow fit. They hold down jobs, raise families, take care of business—they do it all. People who know them might have no idea that anything is amiss. They do their best—they always have. But there is little joy in any of it.

> I truly want to be a person of worth. Anxiety and worry are constant companions, affecting sleep patterns and other things. . . . I truly don't want to let anyone with expectations of me to be let down by a less than excellent effort at the

performance of perceived duty. It's arguably a conundrum
of my own making, and so it's a life journey to undo that
personal Gordian knot and rely on a loving and merciful, not
to mention omniscient and omnipresent, all-powerful God.

— CAROL

Anxiety and worry are much more constant in their
attentions to these souls than serenity and delight have
ever been. They might not ever have thought of describing
themselves as depressed—even the term may be foreign to
them. They might never have sought treatment for it, might
consider any suggestion that they do an insult. They are not
aware that there is any way through life other than the bleak
path they have always walked.

Depression has been a tenant in my life for a long, long time.
Not the *huge* depression some have but the daily visitor who
is there when I wake up until I go to sleep. The hardest part
of this depression is that you don't know what is wrong so you
can't get help. It took me fifty-four years to figure it out.

— RUTH

This book explores depression in the many people of
faith who have experienced it. It cannot claim to do so
fully: like all human experience, depression fits itself to the
vessel it has chosen, and no two of us are the same. No two
courses of healing are ever quite the same, either: one size

definitely does *not* fit all. The uniqueness of depression's mark on each soul can perplex and even annoy the people who love someone suffering from it, and want very much to help. They research remedies: *Didn't she try that doctor I told her about? Why didn't that new drug work? Did he follow up on that herbal thing I showed him? Didn't she read that book I gave her?*

> One of my toughest challenges is the ignorance of well-meaning people who are close to me but can't understand the depression as an actual physical as well as mental problem. They keep trying to "fix it" or me. When I have a relapse even though I am taking my meds as usual and I talk to my nearest and dearest I am totally talking to a brick wall. Why do you think it is so hard for people to comprehend? I become frustrated and so do they. When I really have a bad day and can hardly move out of bed I just want the world to go away.
>
> — FRANCES

They try to be so careful of what they say. For months. For years, maybe. *I don't want to say something that makes her feel any worse*, they tell themselves. After a time, though, they get tired of walking on eggs: something small and annoying happens, and they snap off a peevish remark. They suddenly realize that they've actually been angry at this sad figure in their lives for quite a while, at the very same time as they were just as full of worry. *Damn it!* they say, *Life is tough. It's tough for everyone. You've got it pretty damn good compared to some people. Get over it.* It actually felt good to say this out loud, they reflect later, a little surprised at themselves for having done it. And, besides, it probably didn't hurt the depressed person. I mean, she didn't *say* anything.

Lord, have mercy.

BY THE WATERS OF BABYLON

The journey took forever, it seemed,
over wide valleys, smooth with wear,
over high hills, the occasional mountain, carefully,
across bridges over chasms with various ugly creatures
in them.
When I got to the river,
it bubbled, swaying its way to the ocean
a rhythmic flow
and I lay down in the deep fine grass
hands outspread and thought I was
in the promised land.
But, like Moses, I was on the other side
the wrong side
I looked over and knew it instantly,
knew the irrevocable nature of location, humanity,
physical being
had put me there after long journeys, with people
following blindly
and I could not get to the right side.
And folks on the other side were dancing
a celebration of their river and their view.

(Continued)

The river flows inside me.
Always there, rhythmic, determining the tempo of my days,
Occasionally leaping its boundaries to remind me
in inconsolable pain that I am forever on the wrong side.

—ELOISE BLANCHARD[1]

JESUS WEPT

CHAPTER 1

JESUS WEPT

At first, I didn't know I was depressed. I thought I was just religious.

I knew I was beyond tired, beyond exhausted. I knew I was out of shape. I knew I was overworked. What I didn't know was that there was any way *not* to be any of those things. But then, part of depression *is* not knowing things can be other than the way they are. *This is horrible*, you think, *but I cannot change it. I have always been here and I always will be here. I can't leave*. Maybe there are little things you can do to make life more livable, but the basics are set, and the basics are not good. This is how things look from the trough.

In my office, a beautiful womblike room with wine-red walls and dark wood and stained glass windows, I tried to create an oasis of beauty and quiet that would calm and nurture others, and might even calm and nurture *me*. I bought bunches of roses at the corner vegetable stand and arranged them in clear, round bowls of clean water. I lit scented candles, whose tiny flames reflected and multiplied in the facets of their crystal holders. I rocked in the wooden rocking chair. I played the chants of medieval monks and nuns, the music of Bach. Once in a while I played the Beatles, or something by Paul Simon. Not often, though: they reminded me too painfully of the confident young woman I was when those songs were new, and that young woman just didn't understand. *Get over it*, she said, dismissively.

I sneaked out the back door of the church and across the street to the chiropractor. *Your shoulders are like a rock*, he said every time. *I know*, I would answer. All my muscles were knots of anxious readiness. Readiness for what, I cannot say.

Fourteen, fifteen, sixteen—the heaped-up voicemail messages filled me with dread. Someone wanting something, someone to whom I owed work, someone reminding me of something I had failed to do. "Save," I pressed, over and over. *Save me*, I thought sometimes, and sometimes something dark answered that nobody could save me.

My prayer was the weariness of a child exhausted from too much crying. Prayer in the beautiful wine-colored office was prayer blinking back tears, prayer curiously devoid of hope, prayer even more curiously uninterested in its own outcome. I pressed "Save" and prayed to be saved myself. But I began to suspect that I would not be saved until I left my church and my family and my mind and my body, all the other things I could no longer lift, behind. There was no salvation for me, not here on the earth. The most I could hope for was silence.

And I began to long for that final silence. In my longing, death did not look cold. Or sad. It looked languorous, that motionless end of everything here. Seductive, calling me. I tried it out on my husband, the only person I trusted with such a dark vision.

"I want you to know something about how I feel. It's important to me that you listen."

"OK." He knew of my pain, but did not know what to do about it. Not being able to do anything was hard on him.

"What I have to tell you is that I want to be dead."

He said nothing. He waited.

"I want to stop and not have to start again." He still did not move or speak. This I didn't like. I wanted him to *do* something. I didn't know what it was, but I wanted it. Even now, I still do not know what it was that I wanted him to do.

"Listen, I'm not going to kill myself. I don't want you to think I might do that. I won't." This needed emphasizing.

I was not suicidal: no hoarding of pills, no planning of my own execution, no "ideation." I would not kill myself. But I wanted to *be dead*. Wanted it to *happen* to me. I wanted to be taken out.

"When you're dead," I went on, "you don't have to do anything. You just lie in your box. You're in the ground with earthworms and seeds and other dead people, and you don't know or care. You don't mind. You are quiet." I paused, and then I added, "And your spirit finally knows what it is to be with God, with nothing in the way, and it's a wonderful thing to be with God." I added that religious part almost as an afterthought, although I was pretty sure it was the case. I thought about heaven a lot.

This was a hurtful thing to say to one who loved me deeply. That I wanted to die, that the sweetness of his presence was not sweet enough to make me want to live.

Duty, on the other hand, *was* enough to keep me alive. I had a duty to be alive. I had a duty to him, to my children and grandchildren, to my church. I am not a person who shirks duty. I would not shirk the duty of being alive.

But I didn't have to like it.

At night I lit more candles in crystal holders and eased myself into hot baths of lavender-scented water. The scent of the lavender rose with the steam; the heat of the water eased my aching joints. I took my old prayer book into the bath with me, my wet hands pocking the thin pages with marks of water drops. The ancient words of the Church's daily prayer rose from me, thick with my tears. At other times, I took the same prayers to the chapel, where everything was clean and good, where the sun slanted through the stained glass and pooled rainbows on the floor. There, I often was not alone: another worshipper would join me, and the ancient words were a sweet conversation: "O God, make speed to save us." "O Lord, make haste to help us." *How lovely this is,* I would think as we went back and forth. *How lovely,* as we sang the words antiphonally at Sunday vespers. The depressed often report a loss of the experience of beauty, a flatness that covers everything once held dear and colors it grey. That was not my experience: rarely in my life has the beauty of prayer, of art, of music, of *everything* been more vivid to me than during those painful days. And rarely have I been so unable to derive anything from it beyond the ache of my own isolation. It was as if I beheld intense beauty through an impenetrable window of thick glass. I could not tear myself away from the loveliness, but neither could I myself become lovely.

The tomb of my misery barricaded itself against the persistent rapping of my anger at its door. *No, I am not angry.* Sorrow was august, but anger was unacceptable. But a tic-like drumming of my clenched hand against my right thigh when someone irritated me became more and more frequent. "Stop that!" my daughter ordered when she saw me. "Do you know how you look when you do that? If you're mad, just say so." Mad? *Moi?* My anger was silent, or so I thought. In reality, it was getting louder: my voice more clipped, my tolerance of small inconveniences more slim, my strange beating of myself more obvious to others, more self-mutilating than before. It cannot have been a comfortable thing to see.

I will get up and take a walk in the morning, I promised myself each night. The endorphins generated by walking will help me feel better. Then I will have some energy. But my eyes flew open at ungodly hours—two, three. I would creep from our bed and take up residence in the guest room, tuning the radio to the BBC. Only the Brits and I were up at that hour. I would lie there in the scented dark—more candles—and listen to the cricket scores until I fell asleep. And then, at the normal waking time, I could not arise until it was time to go to work. I worked all day, every day. I worked from early morning until late at night. I worked and slept and woke up to listen to the cricket scores and slept again, fitfully. And then I arose and went back to work.

It seemed necessary, all this working. Necessary, but it seemed also to do little good.

My desk was covered with ineffectual piles of unmet obligations; one was dispatched only at the expense of another, and none were ever satisfied. I gave hurried lip service to healthy-minded ideas about what the clergy should do: they should take time for themselves, they should have a life outside the parish, they should get enough rest, they should take a sabbatical. But the "shoulds" in each of these unexceptionable recommendations rang in my ears louder than anything else, drowning out any grace they might have offered me. All of their gentle counsels took their places among the mountains of my unmet obligations. They felt no different from any of the others. Beyond the feeble palliation of stolen massages and scented baths and candles in crystal holders, my behavior gave not the slightest indication that I understood anything at all about self-care.

Oddly, so oddly that it can only have been by the grace of a loving God—who must by now have regarded me and those entrusted to my care with real alarm—my desperate condition ordinarily did not get in the way of my doing many people genuine good. From somewhere in its depths I daily summoned reserves of empathy and patience beyond what made any sense at all. I managed to preach with power. Looking back, I recall now that many of my sermons *were* about dying and going to heaven. Too many. And they were too heartfelt. That, and the surreptitious beatings

I endured at my own hand, would have been signs of my distress to anyone who knew the code. But few people did. And I certainly wasn't talking.

We will be true to Thee 'til death, we all sang one summer Sunday morning at the end of the 9:30 service. Another hymn about martyrdom, a favorite of mine. Something was strange, though: the room seemed to be concentrated in a tunnel ringed with black. Everything seemed to have slowed down. I sank to the floor at the chapel steps. *I'll just rest.* For how long? A minute? A year? Eventually, I awakened, covered with my own vomit and surrounded by a circle of frightened faces, protesting only weakly when the emergency medical services came to cart me away and not at all when a cardiologist who was suddenly *mine* cleaned out a blocked artery in my heart as casually as he would have unstopped a kitchen drainpipe.

Oh. *That's* what's wrong. I have a heart condition. Neat and clean, a heart condition—except for the vomit. Physical and, it later turned out, electrical as well. Arrhythmia. Medicines for it, lots of medicines. Maybe a pacemaker. This was *electrical*. Oh, good.

I would rest. I tried and failed to write—too tired. My pulse was in the thirties—no wonder I was too tired. I read murder mysteries. I dozed through visitors. I slept all night and much of each day. I came home. I sat at the picnic table. It was beautiful and green in the garden. A heart condition. How lovely.

I was back at work in two weeks. The vestry made me promise to moderate my work schedule. *Yes, I will.* And I did. I kept a log of my working hours. I didn't count the telephone work from home, or the fourteen-hour Sundays. *Progress, not perfection,* I told myself cheerfully. I told myself and others that I was slowing down. That was not true. What I was doing was speeding up, slowly.

When the World Trade Center collapsed, though, there was no pretending anymore. All bets were off. Prayer vigils. Food collections—food, and clean socks and eyedrops and stuffed animals, pouring into the church from all sides. We were in New York, and we could get these things to the site, couldn't we? Yes, certainly. Tragedy brings out the best in people, but it also brings out the worst: the drunks got drunker, the crazy got crazier, the needier got needier. All around me, people were either rising magnificently to the occasion, or falling apart. Some were doing both.

Interestingly, *I* felt better. Of course I can help. Of course I have time to talk. Of course I will go. Who could stay away? The pile of twisted metal and plastic and paper and dust, of hidden bits of human flesh and bone rose high above the ground and went down many stories below it. Workers swarmed over it like ants. The train stations and construction fences wore papers with color photocopies of the missing: *Maybe she became confused and wandered off, and at this very minute maybe she is somewhere in this city, huddled with other amnesiac WTC office workers around a rusty trash can with a fire burning in it to keep them all warm. Maybe.* Maybe. Because you can't disprove the negative, can you?

This was terrible. It was so terrible that my own darkness became irrelevant, a grandiose bid for neurotic attention. *Don't you know what's happened here? How can you even think about your own despair at a time like this?* And I didn't. Not me. And—again by the grace of a loving God, who sighed and used even me—I and the people of God with whom I lived and worked put our shoulders into helping, all of us, became part of the greatest outpouring of human kindness New York had seen in a long, long time.

My adversary just waited. It knew I was no match for it, that it didn't matter how important my important work was. It knew its patience would be rewarded, but I did not know. I thought I was better. It was good to have a sense of purpose again. Good to feel effective. Good to know there were concrete, exhausting tasks on which to spend myself. Good to lead. Good to be *good*. Vestry records from those months show that I reported that I was completely healed, that I was my old self now. The drug of care for others coursed through my veins—I see now that it was a hallucinogen. It allowed me to believe that I was fine. I was anything but fine.

Because I could not allow myself to acknowledge my own hidden pain, my body once again did the honors. Another collapse: I began to stammer slightly during the announcements, saw the same tunneling blackness, said that I needed to sit down, looked without speaking at the same alarmed faces and allowed myself to be led away.

Nobody was buying my lies now. I had not slowed down like I said I would. I had attempted to bury my disease in the dry leaves of my frantic performance, in the embroidery of my duties. More heart medicine. More reassuringly technical scans and tests. And something else, now: medicine that would insinuate itself into the chemistry of my brain, that would tamper with my own way of interpreting what happened in my world. The juice of joy was in short supply among the neurons; the medicine would help me make more. Imagine.

The heart thing was real. I had a real blocked artery. The arrhythmia was real, too. Dangerous things, both of them. But I know that the real reason I could not continue was the crushing weight of unacknowledged despair I carried with me everywhere. I believe that my body's wisdom triumphed over my mind's denial so that I could live, and

I believe that I would have died if my body had not given out and given up. I never would have killed myself, but I would have seen to it that the church killed me. Had it been left to me, I never would have stopped. And I would be dead now.

And I am not dead. I am alive. My life has changed dramatically. I have said good-bye to people and things I hated to leave, chief among them that brave, funny little church and all the beloved people in it. I have told the truth about what I can and cannot give. Sparingly, I have even told it out loud, in public, and have been rewarded for that judicious sharing by the answering stories of many other good and faithful people who have battled my old enemy, too. *You're depressed?* one of them will ask, seeming a bit surprised that I would own up to such a thing in front of people, and I answer with a firm *Yes*. That's probably the most useful thing I say to anyone there.

CHAPTER 2

A LEARNING EXPERIENCE

Religious people want there to be meaning in everything. Randomness is hard on us: that things just happen for no reason sometimes brings us closer than we want to be to the possibility that we're not central to much of anything, and most of us are still too wedded to our ancient anthropocentrism to give *that* up. We still can't help thinking it's all about us. And so we hope and expect the universe to have a message for us. *Let there be something just for me,* we pray and we expect, *something that will make it all make sense. A plan.*

And yet, the crushing weight of depression lies precisely in the meaninglessness that characterizes it. A flat voice within contradicts every hopeful thought: live with it long enough, and the hopeful thoughts don't even bother surfacing. Muffled and parched, bereft of any vision that might ratify your journey or give it a reasonable goal, you trudge on and on for no particular reason other than that you know you're supposed to.

But then, when it lifts: Air! Light! Human company that neither infuriates nor drains, an actual sense of your own humanness! You are in the human race again, after your unexplained absence. Perhaps you were a really good actor, and nobody knew you were gone. But you knew.

After that lift, the person of faith begins to analyze, perhaps. *What on earth was that,* I asked myself after my first episode had begun to lift. Even now, I shiver at the memory of it. I don't ever want to feel that way again.

Still, I think about it a fair amount, that ordeal, that deliverance. I read the book of Exodus and, for a change, I am not repelled by the bloodthirstiness of Exodus 15:21, the oldest couplet in the Bible: *Sing to the Lord, for he has triumphed gloriously! The horse and its rider has he hurled into the sea!* Take *that!* And *that!* A battle has been fought for the sweet nectar of my life, and God has won it. To see and love the colors of things again, to smell the air's deliciousness. No longer to awaken exhausted, disappointed not to wake up dead. To think myself beloved and lovable—sort of lovable, anyway. Lovable in a sole-survivor-of-a-terrible-plane-crash, I-must-be-here-for-a-reason kind of way.

To feel the return of meaning. Now I begin to think that there *was* meaning in all that meaninglessness. I read John of the Cross, again—yes, now I am a little bored by the dense stateliness of his prose, but now I seem to remember that I, too, must have known the love of God in my darkest hour. Yes, I seem to remember it now, I'm sure of it. In memory, I begin to arrange the memory of my deadness so that it will look more like life. I'm not lying or "spinning"— it's just that Providence is ordinarily seen in hindsight.

Or maybe I *am* spinning. Sometimes I wonder about that. Maybe I'm selling myself to myself. Maybe it's all marketing.

Of course, my faith tradition proffers a tempting tray of various delicacies, any number of interpretations for the experience of depression that will fit categories the faith already has. It suggests demon possession as a possible theme—literal or metaphorical demons, take your pick. I had a demon, and it has been exorcised. A satisfying image, this: a stern Jesus rebukes the unclean spirit, who issues from the top of my head or out of my mouth, a malignant little dark angel, like in medieval paintings, and it flies angrily away. But then I remember something in scripture about exorcism, something sobering—what was it? Ah, here it is:

> When the evil spirit comes out of a man, he passes
> through waterless places seeking rest; and finding
> none, he says, "I will return to my house from which
> I came." And when he comes, he finds it swept and put
> in order. Then he goes and brings seven other spirits
> more wicked than himself, and they enter and dwell
> there. And the last condition of that man becomes
> worse than the first.
>
> —LUKE 11:24–26 (RSV)

And I remembers what the shrink has told me many times: the disease of depression is progressive. Attacks subsequent to the first one are often more severe. The pain is a memory now, but that thought can still produce a shudder. *I don't ever want to feel like that again.*

Or perhaps that frightful era just past wasn't a demon at all. Perhaps it was a teaching tool, a means by which I was strengthened in wisdom about the very nature of the human self. Was it *purposed* to teach me about my many blessings by allowing me to experience their privation, in case I ever started taking them all for granted? In truth, I *have* been educated by having survived depression, by the memory of its dreadful emptiness. I do feel glad just to breathe the air without feeling its dead weight on my chest. I do have a more nuanced view of God than a simple equation of God's presence with my own well-being, not that I had ever put much stock in that equation anyway. And it certainly has taught me what a blessing "normal" is. *I don't ever want to feel like that again.*

There is abundant devotional writing about the teaching purpose of suffering, and I can't stand any of it. I didn't think the World Trade Center bombing or the Indian Ocean tsunami or the Sichuan earthquake were sent by God to teach human beings who's boss, and I've never seen my own life story that way, either. I am far from being offended by the randomness of human suffering—I would be troubled by its opposite number, a God willing to rain down horrors on humanity in order to instruct us. It's one thing to acknowledge that we learn from suffering, quite another to believe that God sends it for that reason. I am content to derive what wisdom I can from events in their aftermath. I don't need for God to have planned it all in advance.

Julian of Norwich prayed for suffering so that she might know the love of Christ: "There came into my mind with contrition . . . a desire of my will to have by God's gift a bodily sickness, and I wished it to be so severe that it might seem mortal. . . . In this sickness I wanted to have every kind of pain, bodily and spiritual, which I should have if I were dying, every fear and assaults from devils, and every other kind of pain except the departure of the spirit."[1]

I was in seminary when the modern Julian boom began, and I read the medieval saint's *Showings of Divine Love* several times in those days. But you don't really *have* to pray for suffering, I mutter to myself as I take my old copy of *Showings* down from the bookshelf. You don't even have to put a nickel in. Suffering just *comes*.

I go back and read some more: "For I understood that because of the tenderness of the sweet hands and the sweet feet, through the great and cruel hardness of the nails the wounds grew wide, and the body sagged because of its weight, hanging there for a long time, and the piercing and scraping of the head and the binding of the crown, all clotted with dry blood, with the sweet hair attaching the dry flesh to the thorns, and the thorns attaching to the flesh."[2]

Yikes. I'd forgotten just how graphic Julian could be.

Of course, a person could *prepare* for suffering, which is really what Julian was doing. In her century. In her way. One could prepare a place for it in one's own spiritual narrative—different from praying for the thing itself, maybe, but maybe not so terribly different.

And surely one could *notice* the unfairness of misfortune, in advance of its appearance, *notice* its essential unrelatedness to human deserving one way or the other, and get most of the *Why me?* stuff out of the way ahead of time. One could give some serious thought to one's own future, one's own death, even, and acknowledge that it will surely come. And in that, one might even find a certain ease: after all, much of pain is really panic—about half of what we experience as pain is really shock and surprise. That is why people with chronic pain can endure: it is no *surprise* to them, only the familiar old enemy with whom they live daily. One can ease some of that pain simply by getting ready for it. Which is not at all the same thing as *steeling* oneself for it, becoming an anxious coil of readiness, not at all the same thing as worrying oneself to death about things in advance of their occurrence. Preparing for suffering is admitting to oneself that pain will come into one's life, as it comes into everyone else's. An exception will not be made in my case. So that when pain knocks at my door, I won't be peeking out fearfully through the keyhole, wondering who it is. I'll already *know* who it is. *Oh, it's you,* I'll say. *I was wondering when you'd show up.*

So, then, one's own periods of spiritual deadness, too: why not prepare for them in the same way? Why not admit in advance that they will come, and prepare a place for them in the narrative of one's life, so that their arrival is more like that of an unwelcome in-law than like one's own personal *tsunami*. Some casseroles can be partially prepared in advance, and then finished and baked when it's time to take them to the church potluck supper. Maybe human suffering is a casserole like that.

For some reason, this thought gives me immense comfort. I love to cook.

An e-mail comes from a friend whose lifelong cyclical depression has been resistant to any medication:

> I have come to look at my depressive episodes as learning experiences. No, this is not easy to do, and I am in no way pious about it. It sucks to be in it, and is such a relief to come out of it that I am always grateful to have made it through. What I have learned over the years is to not fight it. I can't do anything to shorten the course except pay attention to the symptoms, get plenty of exercise, sleep in a balanced manner, and talk to my partner. Most of that doesn't stop the process, but it helps me to get through it. I have to remind myself to be gentle with me.
> —ILEEN

I am drawn to the stories of other sufferers, I find. I buy every book about depression that comes out. I'm also on the lookout for famous people's breakdowns, past and present. These, too, are comforting: people of certified worth and substance, eminent actors, scientists, writers like me, only famous and universally respected. How shameful a thing can my depression be if I am in such august company?

And, of course, there are the not-so-famous sufferers I've encountered every day for decades. Nobody gets through thirty years of parish ministry without seeing the effects of depression on individuals and families many times. Every parish priest needs a good rolodex: who are the competent therapists in the area? And who are the loonies I should avoid? What agencies can connect uninsured clients who need psychotherapy but cannot pay the going rate?

And then there is the task of helping people take the first step of agreeing to see a psychotherapist at all. It can take months of patient listening to help a person view this as anything but shameful. Sometimes they react to the suggestion that they could use professional help as if they had been accused of a crime, as if the presence of a psychic illness invalidated all their experience and all their competence. I'm not crazy, they say indignantly.

Well, neither am I, I have learned to answer, *and I've been in psychotherapy many times. I see a therapist now. In fact, you've never known me when I wasn't in therapy.*

I find my way to others who have also taken this bitter journey. Being in New York helps, of course; there, almost everyone either sees a therapist or *is* one. Carefully, I have "outed" myself to colleagues who, I know, have been down the same road. Their company is ironic balm. It is helpful to laugh, to make darkly subversive depression jokes, like the one about being the piece of shit in the center of the universe, with someone who will not be shocked by the language.

That's one thing about depressed people: we can be tedious company sometimes, it's true, but some of us can be pretty funny, too, even when we're in fairly rough shape. With each other (anyway) we have learned (sometimes, at least) a life-saving skill: laughing out loud together about things we used to cry about alone.

WORRY

How many times I heard this advice
from my mother: "Don't worry so much."
In childhood worry made me fearful
of polio and wetting the bed at camp.
It made me lie awake and listen in bed
to the ticking clock and the creak
of the stairs outside my room.
Worry kept me from teenage sex.
In college it made me dread
each new semester and term papers.
Worry would not let me learn
how to ski downhill or scuba dive.
It terrified me when my children
had the croup and were vaccinated
for the first time. Worry teases me
now about my fate—heart attack,
cancer, stroke? Even tonight
worry wraps her long legs around me,
promises to be mine forever.

—HENRY LANGHORNE[3]

CHAPTER 3

I JUST DON'T FEEL ANYTHING

"I had seen the smoke from the 7 train in Queens as I headed into the city that morning. Nobody knew what it meant yet. Someone noticed and pointed it out. 'Look at all that smoke!' I didn't pay much attention."

Like everyone else, Jennifer knew where she was on 9/11, the uncertain Pearl Harbor of the infant new century: she was seeing to some final arrangements for a trip out of town with an old flame, one of a fairly long line of disastrous boyfriends she had collected over the years. The trip never happened, of course. The only thing in the air in those days was World Trade Center dust and the Air Force.

Like everyone else in the days that followed, Jennifer listened to people's stories about where they were, what they thought and felt, who they knew in the two buildings, how they had almost been at the Trade Center that day and then had a doctor visit, an early off-site meeting, a sick child, some last-minute reason not to go. Jennifer *hadn't* been supposed to go there or anywhere near there, *never* went to the World Trade Center, didn't know anybody in the buildings, had survived unscathed by the tragedy about which everyone couldn't seem to stop talking, not even for a minute. The sad stories piled on top of one another like the autumn leaves that were beginning to fall from the trees, and with each one an unpleasant feeling grew in her: not horror, not sorrow, not compassion—something more like *irritation.*

Why couldn't I have died a hero instead of being left with my messed-up life and a sense of futility?

She didn't want to hear the stories. Didn't want to sing "God Bless America" in church, for heaven's sake—walked out when they did that. Didn't want to feel guilty about not having had her life turned upside down, about her largest inconvenience having been missing a trip with an out-of-date *amour.* Something else beckoned, the only thing she wanted to feel: what she wanted was numbness.

> I felt best when I felt nothing. Numb. Numb allowed me to function at work, to continue paying my bills, feeding the homeless, numb allowed me to get through each day without having to think about my life, or my decisions (past or future).

I can say this now in retrospect, because I understand that's what was going on. I certainly didn't recognize it then. I talked with my spiritual director about what I wasn't feeling. She reminded me that I had had a similar reaction when my mother had died. I had functioned for a long time on autopilot before I finally broke down and cried. I accepted her interpretation because it also let me off the hook. I would grieve in my own way in my own time.

We sat in my office as Jennifer reported her lack of emotion to me. There was a touch of defiance in her voice as she told me what it was like to feel nothing at a time like this, a slight, silent daring of me: *Just try and make me feel this. . . .*

Her psychic numbness was a splint, it seemed to me. It protected her from the rawness of her horror at the randomness of what had occurred, its awful unrelatedness to people's deserving, hers or anyone else's. Of course, it also rendered her unable to experience the stern tug at her sleeve of her repentance about her own life. So it was temporarily useful, but not permanently so. You don't splint your broken limb forever. It's just a thing you do while you're waiting to get it set, so it can start healing for real.

She drank more than usual. A lot more, sometimes, she says now. And she found that she couldn't seem to *light* anywhere, not for very long. Didn't seem able to stay in one place, whether it was out with people for dinner or over at her best friend's apartment. People's earnestness about things in those days was irritating.

The only time I felt normal was when I was working in the breakfast feeding program. Jennifer had been volunteering there for several years. The guests there didn't stop getting hungry just because the World Trade Center was bombed by a bunch of lunatics in airplanes. In they came, every Sunday, just as they always had, and serving them was a thing she could *do,* a steady need unrelated to our new tragedy. They didn't talk much about 9/11, the guests. They didn't talk about it at all, really, and this was just fine with Jennifer.

She didn't volunteer down at Ground Zero, although dozens of people she knew did, dishing up hot food, handing out sandwiches, socks, eyedrops, chocolate chip cookies, making coffee for the recovery workers. She just stayed with the feeding program. Her friends all came back from down there excited, talking wonderingly about how New Yorkers had come together over this, and *in such a beautiful way!* That same irritation began to rise from somewhere from within Jennifer's numbness: *People have been getting hungry in New York for a long time,* she told me, with a bitter little laugh. *Wonder where all these folks were then.*

Jennifer treasured her numbness for a long time—as long as it took. If it is true that all our past horrors return to visit us every time a new one comes along, then it's probably true that all our old coping methods come back, too. That was the case with Jennifer—I remembered talking with her about what it had been like when her mother died, of how frozen she had been inside then, and how long it had lasted.

Was this depression, brought on by shock? Maybe so. And *was* it a splint? It's intriguing to think that there might be a *use* for that dreadful numbness, the perverse preference for stasis that characterizes depression. In that state, we cannot and will not move. But perhaps a part of us is broken then, and maybe moving is the last thing we should do. Maybe sometimes numbness is just what the doctor ordered.

Except that the doctor never orders it. The inability to feel pain or pleasure is a symptom, as far as most people in the healing professions are concerned. Nobody in the business seems to think it's a splint; they want to cure it ASAP. I wonder, though: a period of psychic numbness seems to have served Jennifer rather well, and to have served her well through two traumatic events. It gave her some time to heal underneath it, and she did heal. Maybe it's just her way.

On occasion, platoons of psychotherapists were delivered to various spots during the recovery effort—a bunch of them appeared at the morgue one day, I heard. I wonder how *that* went: the morgue could be a busy place in those early days. The theory at the time was that people who've been traumatized need to talk about their feelings immediately or terrible things will happen to them. But Jennifer didn't do that—she stayed in her splint until it was time for her to come out, and she did that at her own pace, which was a slow one.

Although she did not seek psychotherapy, Jennifer did not heal alone. Besides her spiritual director, she began to grow closer to a group of nuns, and to spend more time at their convent. Eventually, she went to live in the convent with an eye to discerning whether she might have a vocation to that order, and after a time she was clothed as a novice. Today she is a life-professed sister. And she still volunteers one day a week in the same feeding program.

So: a religious vocation as a cure for depression?

No, I don't think so. I know far too many depressed nuns and monks to recommend *that*. It's a hard life, and will always be a minority lifestyle.

But depression as a splint, enabling the spirit to rest and gain enough strength to live fully again? Maybe so, sometimes. Maybe the very numbness symptomatic of this clinical condition of despair is a means toward its healing. That would be elegant indeed.

And it would be absolutely counter to the mantra I have told everyone who cared to listen since my own most serious depression: *I don't ever want to feel that way again.* But what if that's the way my soul catches up with my history? What if it's part of the way in which the self regroups? What then?

My friend Charlie thinks it is. His description of his own depression sounds awfully familiar: "Slowly the world began to look gray and colorless. I began to sleep late and had little energy. Then I entered that realm where I would hear myself and others as if from a distance. I became an observer of life, but a disengaged observer. Every task took extra energy; joy and excitement were faded memories."[1]

Charlie was like me, except that my depression was in color, while his was in black and white. But his eventual assessment of its use in his life reminds me of Jennifer's therapeutic numbness and makes me wonder about myself: "I had been totally absorbed in coping with one crisis after another. . . . Even though I had experienced growth and arrived at a resolution, I still needed time to stop the roller coaster and process it all. . . . I required respite and psychic withdrawal time. I do not believe all depressions are the same. Some seem to be purely caused by a chemical imbalance, while others are initiated by a psychological conflict or trauma. All, however, have a spiritual component that is important to honor."[2]

What if that's so? What if some depression has a healing, consolidating *mission* in the life of the one to whom it comes? Then wouldn't the very last thing that person needs be a pill that enables him to go on as before? Wouldn't that be like filling yourself up with painkillers so you could walk on your broken ankle?

Oh, dear.

Now, a familiar, absurd stab of shame: I take a pill to ease my psychic desperation. I seem to need it; without my antidepressant, I succumb to pervasive feelings of worthlessness and hopelessness, become prone to great irritation and annoyance, for no good reason. I don't have these sorrows now—although they lurk on the periphery of most of my days, as if waiting for their moment of opportunity, and I can see them out of the corner of my eye. Certainly I do not miss their bitter centrality in my life. But what if I'm denying myself my splint by easing my pain? What if my pain is *useful* to me in some way, of which I am unaware? Am I circumventing a process I need? Impatient with my own God-given healing mechanism because I don't recognize it as such?

Or am I just appropriately caring for myself in order to live life more fully?

Don't be an idiot, my friend Jay tells me at dinner. *Why do you keep stewing about it? You'd take insulin if you were diabetic, wouldn't you?*

I can't count the times I've said exactly that to people who were to-ing and fro-ing about taking psychotropic medications—not the idiot part, I mean, just the part about the diabetes. I never cease to be amazed at the fact that often I can help someone else do something I can't help myself do. I've been taking this medicine for almost a decade, and have been scolding myself about it off and on the whole time. One thing: we depressed people are pretty boring when you get to know us. We keep having the same conversations with ourselves, over and over again, even when we're in decent shape.

I am now in my thirty-eighth year of taking an antidepressant medication for a brain-imbalanced depression. This happened to me somewhere in menopause when I was approximately thirty-eight years old. I am now seventy-six years old. The drug I take has worked well for me, and without it I become suicidal in the extreme. . . . I have talked about this to friends and have found out how embarrassed and humiliated some people feel about their

ailment. It is as though we are still back in the Dark Ages
discussing mental problems or that the problem is of our
making. Ask me anything you want; I am a talker and not
shy about my condition. The more I can help people, the
more I will talk.

    —RITA

The fear that easing the pain of depression will somehow deprive us of a necessary important spiritual season in
our lives is not particularly well-founded. Here is the late
psychiatrist and mystic Gerald May on this very fear:

> There is a persisting notion in some circles that the
> medications used to treat depression and other psy-
> chiatric illnesses can somehow interfere with deeper
> spiritual processes such as the dark night [of the soul].
>
>   Nothing could be further from the truth. To my
> mind, there is never an authentic spiritual reason to
> let any illness go untreated. . . . I am not certain why
> people still think that medication can interfere with
> God's work in human souls. Perhaps it is because
> medications are frequently abused and sometimes
> substituted for the spiritual consolations people seek.
> Or perhaps it is the memory of older psychiatric medi-
> cations that accomplished little but sedation. More
> likely, it is probably due to the persisting ancient dual-
> ism between matter and spirit—that things of the flesh

like chemicals can have nothing but a negative effect
on the "higher" things of the spirit. In order to believe
this, though, one's theology would have to hold that
God's grace is so weak and ineffective that a chemical
compound can block it.[3]

This helped. Maybe the numbness of clinical depression *is* a splint, sometimes. Maybe it does keep us still for a
time, when stillness is exactly what we need. But only for
a season. Nobody needs a lifetime of catatonia. There is
no good reason not to reach for whatever healing you can
while the splint is on, because healing was the only reason
you reached for the splint in the first place. Any healing that
happens underneath it, by whatever means it happens, is a
godly thing indeed.

CHAPTER 4

TROUBLE IN PARADISE

We sat across from each other in a restaurant. Everything about him was sad: his face a grim mask, his eyes full of unshed tears, his body still as death. Only his lip trembled, just a little bit. I'd have missed it if I hadn't known to look.

Don't you think you should see somebody? I asked. *A therapist?* He had just told me of his despair. He shook his head. *I could never witness to anybody again if I were in therapy. I'd feel like a fraud.*

"Witnessing" is telling the story of how God came into your life. Ultimately, it's supposed to be a happy tale—although you're allowed many trials and snares along the way, it needs to end with you surrendering yourself to God and accepting Jesus Christ as your Personal Savior, and then things are supposed to be all right with you.

You're not supposed to be hopeless and want to die. That may mean that you were mistaken in thinking that you had really surrendered. It may mean that you were lying. Who knows what else it could mean? There's not a lot of room in this narrative for despair. So people committed to it who find themselves staring despair in the face tend to keep that fact to themselves.

This conversation took place years ago—decades, actually. It was before people were as open about their inner lives as they are today. It took place at a time in the man's life when his religious faith had become very important to him. The style of faith that had grabbed him was that of the charismatic renewal, the movement within the church that embraced the gifts of the spirit, including healing, prophecy, and speaking in tongues. It had a lively sense of the living presence of Christ in the world, and expected to see signs of that presence. Like this young man, many people had rediscovered the faith in which they were raised and felt it quicken to vivid new life. He was a natural leader, although he may not have known that as well in those days as he knows it now. People in his prayer community turned to him for wisdom and sanity. His dry humor was mildly famous.

But the culture of the prayer groups he frequented and the things he read expected to see a fairly immediate relationship between faith and spiritual well-being. It ought to feel good to be a Christian, they felt. The songs they sang were all happy praise songs about the joy of loving Jesus, and their understanding of scripture tended toward the literal. They were committed to healing prayer and excited about miracles of healing that had happened in their midst. They had the gift of seeing God everywhere.

Or almost everywhere. The people in the prayer group—and it was a large one, several hundred at the weekly meeting—drew a sharp distinction between The Spirit and The World. They had ample scriptural justification for this, they believed—the Gospel of John was a favorite, with its powerful imagery of darkness and light, its larger-than-life Jesus striding magnificently through the events of his life and his death, seemingly untouched by any of them—choosing not to emphasize the fact that in John, alone among the four gospels, we see a Jesus who weeps when his friend dies. The teachings given at the regular meetings were often about how to resist the world, about its lures and temptations, about how the categories of the world were nothing like the categories of the Kingdom.

Nobody in the prayer group ever talked about depression. They talked about having faith. You needed to believe that God would handle everything. It was but a short walk from there to the idea that if your healing was a result of your faith, then your continuing illness must be due to your lack of it. This came dangerously close to the feelings the young man was having already: guilt about the very fact of his desolation.

He may have felt isolated, but he was far from alone. Many people resist turning to their communities of faith with the truth about themselves, for fear that understanding and support will not be forthcoming:

> I am currently on a journey toward becoming a priest. . . .
> With so many people having prejudice against people on
> antidepressants, I don't feel that obtaining a prescription
> while I am "under a microscope" is an option for me
> this time.
>   —VERONICA

Such self-censorship where depression is concerned arises from the fear of rejection by the church, as much as from the fact of it: some people are already so convinced that their condition is shameful that they don't even apply. Others do, and wish they hadn't:

> Spiritually, I survived the church telling me the
> following:
> If I confess my sins, the depression will go away.
> If I was not gay, I wouldn't have this problem with
> depression.

I must be out of right relationship with God.
Pray more.
Have more faith.
You will go to hell if you kill yourself.
It's a demon. We must pray it away.

    —ILEEN

The notion was that if I trusted God enough, had enough
faith, if I really loved Jesus, then I would be fine and my
depression and anxiety would go away. Obviously that didn't
work.

    —DONALD

I did have a spiritual director. Looking back, I don't think
he ever addressed the mental health issues I was facing.

    —TRACEY

Every church you walk into has the image of a man
being tortured and murdered that is much more powerful
than the sense of resurrection. There was so much
emphasis on brokenness that it contributed to my
hopelessness.

    —FAYE

Such a spectrum of woes where church teaching,
practice—even décor—are concerned! No wonder so

many are tempted just to close out the church's account altogether. But there are at least two sides to everything; clinical depression and the church are both manifold enough that there are as many reasons to come as there are to stay away.

People of faith *do* face unique challenges when the neurotransmitters go haywire. Years of teaching—some of it inept—about the joys and comforts of faith and the power of prayer, about the importance of trust in God, about the instructive value of suffering can combine to make them feel that their experience of depression is somehow disloyal to the cause. A profound feeling of worthlessness is a hallmark of the condition as it is; a depressed person really doesn't need the added burden of having somehow disappointed God.

On the other hand, the life of faith brings together unique resources for dealing with the depression and its miseries: a powerful mythology about resurrection and healing, a community that, at its best, enshrines love and welcome to the poor in spirit, an ancient practice of prayer that has taken sorrow seriously for hundreds—thousands—of years. Here is a woman who has suffered paralyzing periods of depression as a part of her bipolar illness:

> My pastors have consistently accepted me when I was
> down and when I was up. They prayed for me and believed

that this was simply something I was going through, not my permanent position. They also worked at improving my self-image by positive reinforcement and prayer. Also, my friend and prayer partner would encourage me and nagged me to activity when I was depressed. She couldn't be rebuffed.

My own prayer suffered. The practice of Bible reading helped. I felt that if I could not pray, at least I could be faithful in reading the word. The numerous opportunities for gathering together in prayer in the church or in house fellowships helped me to continue to be with people when I would prefer to isolate myself.

Has my religious faith hurt me? In some ways, I think my Catholic upbringing and the overemphasis on guilt made me very hard on myself. I had a sensitive spirit and thought I was always doing something bad or wanting to. I think the guilt stuff reinforced my low self-esteem. The concept of mortal sin and going to hell also brought out my all-or-nothing approach. When I was ready to give up on the church, I was ready to give up on God.

—LINDA

Many people, like Linda, seem able to let the church be the mixed thing it is, taking from it what is helpful and taking the rest with a grain of salt. The church is a human institution—yes, it's about God, but it's full of human beings, and they are the ones through whom it became what it is, so it's shaped a lot like we are. It is far from perfect.

Like all your other associations—your marriage, your friendships, your job—it can inhabit your life for good or ill, and who you are has a lot to do with which it will be.

As a priest and spiritual director, I see every day how hard it can be for a person who self-identifies as religious to come to terms with a diagnosis of depression. This is difficult for anyone, of course, but church folk often carry a guilt about their bleakness that slows them down in seeking the professional help they need: they may try to pray it away, and then they feel even worse when they are unable to do so. They sometimes opt for counseling with a kindly clergyperson when what they need is a trained psychotherapist, and too many clergy permit them to do this for too long, in effect helping them to stay sick. If psychotropic medications are prescribed, they are apt to invest the decision of whether or not to use them with a moral freight that does not rightly belong to it.

I travel widely throughout the country and abroad, leading retreats on various topics. In hundreds of such gatherings over the years, bringing together thousands of people, I do not recall even *one* in which the issue of how a person of faith can deal with depression did *not* surface. Depression is an immense public health problem: around twenty million Americans suffer from it—that's almost

10 percent of the population. At some point in their lives, 10 to 25 percent of women and 5 to 12 percent of men will become clinically depressed, affecting the lives of more than three times as many spouses, parents, and children. It is estimated that depression exacts an economic cost of over $30 billion each year in the United States, and that estimate deals with tangible things: lost wages, hospitalization, outpatient therapy, medication. The cost of the human suffering depression causes cannot be measured, but it is vast.

But healing each *case* of depression is small and slow, the delicate work of the soul's healing, partnering with the mystery of brain chemistry and the nourishing experience of being heard and understood.

One of the reasons I know so many stories of people's depression battles is that I sometimes disclose my own battle with it in my talks. I hope that my matter-of-factness about this unhappy fact of my own life demystifies it for my audience, preempting the rush to the Sunday school platitudes that satisfy only people who have never been depressed. I believe that we'd all be better off if we were a great deal more matter-of-fact about depression than we are. I've not known shame to be much help to me or anyone else in getting better from anything, and certainly not from this sickness of the soul.

As full of land mines as the life of faith can be for a depressed person, it also carries with it graceful resources for healing and wholeness for the many people who have struggled against despair while, at the same time, attempting to live a considered moral and ethical life, a life unafraid of mystery and depth. And a little disorder.

THE MAGIC KINGDOM

One of the reasons I love Disneyland (apart from the gardens) is that so much is lifted off of your shoulders. Someone else thought, *Where would a nursing mother go on a hot day?* and came up with air-conditioned nursing rooms, with nannies dressed as Mary Poppins, and a baby restaurant, serving baby food. Someone else thought of people coming through with juggling tricks to keep everyone amused while standing in long lines. I lost my youngest daughter there, mentioned it to a guard, and in fifteen seconds there was a circle of thirty Disney employees holding hands drawing the circle inward; she was found in under a minute, having gone back to look at something fun. I know someone who lost her engagement ring on a ride at Disney and they found it for her.

Is this the Kingdom of God? Is this what we really want?

For me, the answer is no, not for always. I am happy spending time there, but the Magic Kingdom is peculiarly draining, to have so many choices taken away from you. We lived close enough to Anaheim

(*Continued*)

that we always had to go with visiting friends and family. I've been there a lot. At first, it is fun to fall into the flawless and safe routine. Eventually it is stifling.

So, I will accept the craziness of my life, the anxiety, the depression. I will accept the surprises, the choices, and the tragedies. And I will continue to seek to understand the mercies of God.

—Jennifer Zeliff Kearney

CHAPTER 5

CHARGED WITH THE CARE OF SOULS

> When I have been terribly depressed during Holy Week, . . .
> the cloud becomes the very air that I breathe. I go
> through the motions of the liturgies with little, I think,
> obvious disturbance to anyone else, but as though my legs
> are filled with cement, my heart is palpably heavy, and my
> constant good cheer is immensely costly. The theological
> heaviness of the week seems unreal and beside the point.
> I concentrate on breathing and getting through—no real
> reflection, just grind. Jesus, have mercy.
> —MARTY

Note, please, the "constant good cheer." There is nobody who doesn't love Marty. Nobody. He is a born pastor, the most faithful visitor of hospitals and sick rooms I've known in a good while, if ever. Marty is droll, self-deprecating. Marty is consummately loving, with everyone. Marty lights up a room just by entering it. His parishioners adore him; when he left his last parish, he thanked them in his farewell sermon for allowing him to "pray and play" with them for a season, and that's exactly what life was like for them during his years there. Men, women, and children wept through that last service. So did Marty.

Also note, please, how "little obvious disturbance to anyone else" there was. This is important to depressed clergy; we don't want our bleakness to injure anyone, and we're prepared to ignore what we must in order to believe that it doesn't. Having our churches be all right is as close as we think we can get to being all right ourselves, and we won't give up our illusions about that without a fight.

Immensely costly, he calls it. Oh, yes.

Marty visits his spiritual director. He is mordantly funny even in that encounter — Marty is funny everywhere he goes — but at least here he can be brutally honest about his own misery. Currently, he is trying another anti-depressant; it's too soon to tell if it will work or not. Marty is a graduate of several of these, and he knows the drill. Someday soon, we have heard, there will be a blood test by means of which a person will be able to know immediately if an antidepressant will work for him, even before it does, which should help us all endure the fact that so many of them require a wait of weeks or even months before they "kick in."

But we don't have that blood test, not yet, and so Marty must wait and see. Three weeks, six weeks, with no guarantee that the fog will lift. And he can only try one medication at a time. It can take a year to get all this squared away, to find out which one is the silver bullet. And then things can change—a drug that has served you well for years can dwindle suddenly to nothing in its effectiveness, for no apparent reason. The shrink gets out his chart again. Irritable? Sleepless? Brooding? Hopeless? Severe, moderate, mild, or not at all?

The chart helps. Its blandness is oddly reassuring; the uniqueness of our sorry symptoms boils down to some predictable facts on a page. Irritable? Brooding? Somehow it is easier to say *Yup, I'm a moderate in brooding and a severe in sleepless* than it is to walk into someone's office and burst into tears—although I've done that. It helps to know that others have felt this way, enough others that there's a form to fill out about it. *So maybe I'm not from Mars,* we think.

And this person with the chart doesn't seem shocked at us. As we have learned not to be, no matter what comes through our office doors. Ah, this is a fellow professional in the care of souls: coming at it from a different angle, for sure, but recognizably engaged in the repair of the world, bit by bit. As we are. *Maybe I am not such a freak*, we think, relaxing slightly into the armchair across from the therapist's chair. *And maybe I don't have to run this meeting. Maybe I can receive, as well as give.*

We remember how hard that can be for people in our line of work, receiving. How controlling a thing all our giving can be, if we let it become that. How good it looks, all that giving we do! *But beauty is as beauty does*, we think. We know that those charged with the care of souls can do a lot of damage, that if we don't take care of ourselves in the right way, we'll take care of ourselves in the wrong way. We have had colleagues who have done that: had destructive love affairs with parishioners, fallen into alcoholism or dependence on other drugs, flirted with death through overeating and lack of exercise, acting out their unspoken psychic pain in ways that end up rippling pain and betrayal far beyond the boundaries of themselves and their families. We know that the stakes on our well-being are high.

> For me, having a sensitive, kind, caring Superior made it easy to ask if I could see a therapist. She suggested a couple of people I might consider, but left it to me to find the right person. I feel very fortunate and grateful for that—it could have been otherwise. I doubt that many, if any, of the Sisters knew I was seeing anyone, except for those I told and the one who paid the bills—probably most of the Community

didn't see me as depressed—more likely they would have said cranky.

Every antidepressant I've tried has made me sleepy—and that does sometimes make it hard to make a fair contribution to our life, in terms of getting my work done and doing it well, and being where I'm supposed to be, and on time. Sometimes I've struggled with that—and some of the Sisters have come to see me as lazy or unwilling, I think. I would find it hard to understand, too, if I had never taken an antidepressant. Most probably don't even know I take medication, so what else could they think.

Right now I am taking Cymbalta—it's a terribly expensive drug—how does that fit with a vow of poverty? I know the poor, the real poor, endure without that kind of help, without even knowing there is help. Don't ask how I can justify this.

I am a kinder person when I take an antidepressant—I take things in stride that would otherwise have me lashing out in anger. I guess, really, it's just pain relief—other kinds of pain make me irritable, too.

—SISTER MARGARET

Are you taking your day off? I ask Marty on the phone. I'm in Italy and he's in New York, but we talk a lot. I usually call him on Fridays to nag him about his day off. Sometimes he wanders down to the office to take care of some small task, but he knows that I'll yell at him if I find out about it.

We both know from bitter experience that spending all of
our available time at the church can be an early sign of an
impending slide—it begins to seem reasonable to have no
life outside of the church. Having one just seems like too
much trouble, really. It begins to seem easier just to work
until we drop, day after day, and then fall into bed night
after night, so that we can do it all again tomorrow. Soon
our topics of conversation narrow to include only church
business, church problems, church drama. We become all
church, all the time.

The colleague to whom you have given permission to
nag you about respecting your limits is an angel sent from
God. Everybody who works—not just clergy, but everyone
who is tempted to *become* his or her important work—
needs regular contact with a few truth-tellers. People who
know what your work is like. People who have told the same
half-truths to themselves that you have told to yourself. And
they have to love you, too. Do you have a colleague you can
honestly say you love? No? Find one. Go through the list
and pick out the ones you admire and whose company you
enjoy. Have lunch. Cultivate the friendship. Do this now,
for heaven's sake, while you're still relatively OK—so that
when the chips are down and you are scarcely presentable,
you have someone to whom you can turn.

AARON

Holiness on the head,
Light and perfection on the breast,
Harmonious bells below, raising the dead
To lead them unto life and rest.
Thus are true Aarons dressed.

Profaneness in my head,
Defects and darkness in my breast,
A noise of passions ringing me for dead
Unto a place where is no rest.
Poor priest thus am I dressed.

Only another head
I have, another heart and breast,
another music, making live not dead,
without whom I could have no rest:
In him I am well dressed.

Christ is my only head,
My alone only heart and breast,
My only music, striking me even dead;

(*Continued*)

That to the old man I may rest,
And be in him new dressed.

So holy in my head,
Perfect and light in my dear breast,
My doctrine tuned by Christ, (who is not dead,
But lives in me while I do rest)
Come people; Aaron's dressed.

    —GEORGE HERBERT[1]

CHAPTER 6

THE DEFENDANT AS PROSECUTOR

It was a fine New York day in early June: bright sun and blue sky interrupted the permanent dusk of Lower Manhattan, where skyscrapers block much of the light, and people were out on the sidewalk, passing up the subway for a long walk home. I was one of them, and not just because of the weather, either: today I would drop the manuscript of my first book off at the publisher, right on time. It wasn't far, and the weather was so nice. Why not walk?

My favorite route uptown on foot was past the fabric stores on Broadway—not that I sewed that much anymore, but I still loved to look at the bolts of cloth and imagine what wonderful things I might make from them if my life were different. West on Chambers Street and north on Broadway, and there they were, window after window of lovely summer fabrics. This was just about as good as life gets, I thought as I walked and looked: the sun, the city, the people, the fabric, dinner with friends later on, and the manuscript under my arm.

When the car hit me, I didn't know what it was: it came up behind me, jumping the curb right onto the sidewalk, knocking me into the brick wall of the store in whose window I had been admiring the bolts of bright fabric. I do not remember being afraid. Not afraid, and not even quite aware of my pain. I remember that time seemed to slow down and almost stop: an event that can only have taken a second or two seemed to go on and on, the impact on my back to stretch out in time. I collected myself: I would just give myself a shake and continue my walk home, so that my evening could unfold as I had planned.

But one of my legs did not work, it seemed. I stood against the brick wall, trying to take a step, until a man called out to me. *Don't move!* he said. I nodded, and sank to the ground.

No fear. Not much pain, even, if I didn't try to move. But I did feel *something*, and I remember it still, all these years later. What I felt was *shame*.

I felt as if I had done something wrong. As if my own clumsiness had caused this. I felt as if I were malingering, as if this event were somehow an old story. *You're just being dramatic,* a voice from inside me somewhere sneered. *You always do that. You always try to make everything about yourself.*

Clearly, a person who can blame herself for being run down by a car *while on the sidewalk* needs some work.

The summer weeks and months that year were not as I had hoped or expected they would be: I felt the pain of my broken bones soon enough, and some of it is with me still, years later. It was time to begin working on my next book. *Well, this is OK,* I thought about my confinement as I recovered, *After all, I didn't break my wrist! I can get a lot of writing done while I'm home.* But not so: I couldn't focus, found myself staring at a blank sheet of paper, unable to think of anything to write on it. Every night I imagined myself writing the following day, cheerful at my desk by the window, an irresistible vision of productivity. But no. I just sat there and gazed at the river, at the Empire State Building in the distance, at the men toiling in the meat market down below, loading enormous sides of beef onto trucks, trotting back and forth in their blood-stained white butchers' coats. My second book, due at the end of that summer, would be late.

The harsh voice that had scolded me as I lay on the sidewalk badgered me into getting up and back to work at the church in record time. The photographer came and took the photograph for the book cover as I leaned against a brick wall near our apartment, my cane out of sight. My exhausted face stares back at me from underneath my makeup as I look at that book now. I ran up enormous bills taking taxis to work, being unable to manage the subway stairs. And, to my immense shame, I was ineffective once I got there, taking more and more time to do less and less.

I would go from work to physical therapy, where I would push myself harder than they advised and get worse instead of better. Their exercises weren't challenging enough, I thought; *that* was the problem. I decided to augment them—lots of walking. I had read about an injured fighter pilot who walked his way to an early recovery after breaking his back; I would be like him, I decided. I walked to work once, to Lower Manhattan from Greenwich Village, a distance of about two miles. My entire right side was immovable by the time I arrived. It took months to recover from the reinjury.

I was ashamed of this, too. I wanted to rise magnificently above my pain and weakness, like my fighter pilot, and instead I was becoming their prisoner. I wanted to be inspiring, and instead I was pitiable. And with all this, I still felt I was malingering. The harsh voice continued: *You're just lazy. You're just trying to get people's sympathy. You know there's nothing really wrong with you.*

You know, there have been a lot of studies on treating chronic pain with antidepressants, my doctor told me. He had already administered several rounds of steroid injections into my spine, which helped some, and a fairly excruciating treatment involving the injection of sugar into the tendons of my pelvis—the tendons would burn, because of the acid produced by the sugar, and then they would shrink as they healed, holding the bones together more firmly. It is an index of my pain in those days that this project seemed reasonable to me.

The SSRIs have some good clinical experience behind them for pain, he said. *Prozac, Paxil, those drugs. It's something we could try.*

Besides, he went on, *you probably are depressed. Look at what's happened to you.* I was shocked to hear him say this about me, and so casually! Depressed? And I was ashamed again.

But I did take the pills he gave me. Nothing happened for a long time—weeks, maybe a month or more. And then, a miracle: my physical pain was cut in half. At *least* in half: there were days when I had none at all. I was giddy with the freedom of it—it had been so long.

Or maybe I was giddy with something else. The withering voice of my deep self-suspicion was quiet. No more harsh internal lectures about malingering. No more awakening in the wee hours for no reason. Maybe the doctor was right. Maybe it was not only bones and tendons that had cried out in pain. Maybe my spirit did, too, inextricably intertwined with my body and with my brain, including its complex neurochemistry. Here was my history: my lifelong harsh inner voice, my auto accident, my months—years, now—of pain. But that history did not sum me up or determine me, not by itself. Here was also the person in whose life that history happened, a creature of both experience and enzyme, horror and hormone, of trauma and of the titration of minute powerful substances influencing everything about and within me.

Who am I? Who are you? *I don't want to take these drugs,* we say. *I don't want to become somebody other than who I am.* But we are always becoming, every day, all of us: the core of our selves is *mutable.* We like to think it is not, but we are mistaken about that. In and around our own experience we go, taking ourselves with us as we travel, and these portable selves of ours respond to what they see and hear and bathe in. They do not remain the same.

For the Deuteronomic voice of blame to vanish so abruptly was a bit of a shock, once I noticed it was gone. I cannot say that I felt like a different person: I felt like myself. What had changed was my inner harshness, which I only now saw had been with me for a long time, long before my physical injury had happened. I remembered that a wise counselor and friend had noticed it decades before, when I was discerning whether or not I might be called to priesthood. Had remarked on how hard I was on myself. Had given me a maxim to keep, as a warning: *If you love your neighbor and hate yourself,* he said, *God help your neighbor.* Well, yes, that certainly made sense. But I clung to my harshness anyway; could not, would not give it up.

And now, suddenly, things had changed. Things that had seemed out of bounds—a nap in the afternoon, for instance, or a day off—seemed no longer to be such terrible crimes. That snide voice, as old a companion as it was, was not really *me,* I saw. I did not cease to be myself without it. It was as if I had been carrying a valise full of heavy stones, and had finally set it down. I was lighter, freer to move about. It seemed odd to me, and it still does, that a pill, smaller by far than the nail on my smallest finger, would have such an effect. But it did.

It seemed *so* odd that, in fact, that after a time I ceased to believe it was true. I felt fine. My unwonted ease had become my New Normal. And, since the medicine had no discernable "kicking in" effect, no euphoric rush that I could feel and know that it was working, it was easy to convince myself that I didn't need it anymore, that I would be able to maintain my well-being on my own. It must be true, I thought. I felt so *normal.*

And this was something I wanted very much to be. A person, a really *good* person, I thought, should not need a pill to keep from drowning in her own self-loathing. She should be able to give herself a good shake and get her act together. And a religious leader, especially—surely *she* is strong enough not to need psychotropic drugs. Now that she has had a decent spell of normal emotional life, surely she has learned how to be normal.

This has happened several times: I have decided to do without my antidepressant. Each time, my psychiatrist has been less than enthusiastic. *Here is your test from when we began*, he says patiently, pulling out a sheet of paper covered with numbers and circles. This was my introduction to the HAM-D, the Hamilton Rating Scale for Depression. It is an inventory to gauge how depressed ill you are. I take it every few months.

- Trouble sleeping: Severe, Moderate, Mild, Not at all?
- Increase or decrease in appetite: Severe, Moderate, Mild, Not at all?
- Feelings of hopelessness: Severe, Moderate, Mild, Not at all?
- Thoughts of dying?
- Brooding or obsessing thoughts?
- Irritability?

My initial score had been 41 — severely depressed. That was certainly accurate; my memory of those excruciating days is vivid; *I don't ever want to feel that way again, not ever,* I said to my husband, after light had begun to appear at the end of the tunnel. Even now, I shudder to think of it: that leaden spirit, that passive longing to be dead, that harsh inner voice, that desperate, doomed desire to please everyone.

And here you are the last time you stopped the medication. It was a 27 — not as bad as a 41, for sure, but a normal score is 7 to 9. I remember that day: I stumbled into his office and sat down. I told him I thought maybe I needed medication again, and I began to cry.

Today I feel normal. I feel as if I could surely stop this little pill and be just fine. How can such a tiny pill make such a difference in such a large person? But now I know that I have tried it three times and each time I slid back, almost all the way to the bottom. And I don't ever want to feel that way again.

I am wondering about my recurring desire not to take the pills. About my curious insistence that I be "responsible" for my own mood, even when I know that responsibility has little to do with it. In large measure, what happens in depression is chemical in nature, and so the application of a little chemistry can often change it significantly. Three times I have been in the trough of significant despair, and three times I have been helped enormously by medication.

And yet sometimes, even now, I long to be free of this medicine that has helped me so much. All the evidence points one way, and yet I persist in wanting to go the other. I don't long to give up my thyroid medicine or my blood pressure pills—why do I wish I weren't on Lexapro?

It's because I am filled with irrational shame about the reason I am taking it. Shame—the same reason I felt somehow to blame for being hit by a car while standing on the sidewalk. I habitually entertain a scathing attitude toward my own sins and sorrows that I would never hold toward anyone else's. This is my default mode—I have to coach myself not to feel this way. I am a priest who has—many times—encouraged *other* people suffering from depression to consider medication, helped them through *their* feelings of shame about it. And, all the while, I myself fight the same feelings of shame.

A person with a more mythological view of life than I have might be tempted to think that this desire of mine to be free of my medicine was a ploy of the depression demon himself, his attempt to get back into the driver's seat of my psychic life. Or maybe that's not so mythological, after all. Maybe there really *is* a battle going on for possession of my soul, the darkness constantly on the lookout for new ways to sap my strength. The promise of psychotropic drugs carries an odd caveat for religious people: They're wait-ing for the miracle, waiting for their sincere belief in the power of prayer to be vindicated, not sure that feeling good is, by itself, a worthy goal. *Shouldn't I wait for God to act?* And—most of all—they fear that taking a drug will make them into someone else. They don't feel entitled to feel better unless they can "do it themselves."

> I've been told that my depression is most likely brain chemical related and that medication (Prozac) would probably be required. I resisted that assessment for several reasons. I dislike having to take medicine, especially if the side effects are personality altering. . . . Also I mistrust the long term effects of most Western pharmaceuticals. More importantly, I felt/feel that my depression can be handled spiritually with occasional herbal supplements when I recognize the lengthening shadows of approaching darkness.
>
> —JAN

I read that Saint John's wort is the most widely prescribed medication for depression in Europe, I tell the psychiatrist. *What if I tried Saint John's wort?*

I tried the herb for a while, years ago. But who knows? Maybe I'm different now. Maybe it would work this time.

He sighs and looks like he wants to retire. *There aren't very many clinical studies . . .* he begins, but I cut him off.

That's because Saint John's wort isn't made by the drug companies, I tell him, *and they're the ones who fund all the studies.*

I go to the National Institutes of Health Web site and look up Saint John's wort. What I like about it is that it's an herb, not a synthetic. Saint John's wort is natural, like okra or string beans. This fact alone has immense appeal to me, with all my expensive medicine bottles lined up in my dresser drawer.

And what about all those Europeans? Can fifty thousand Frenchmen be wrong? But NIH says it's for the treatment of *mild* depression. All those Europeans are *mildly* depressed, I guess. Mine is not mild, I think, with a familiar remembered stab of shame. After all, I *was* a 41 on the HAM-D.

And I don't ever want to feel like that again.

I am helped and encouraged, though, by people who are much more matter-of-fact about their medication than I am prone to be, and I seek out their witness to help me remember that science and religion are not in opposition to each other. That what science has contributed to human healing *is* part of what God does.

I have come to live into an acceptance of the body, complete with neurochemistry, I was given and that I need to pray that body, here and now.
— BETTY

I finally found my way to an M.D. and medication after several years of real suffering. I could not make life decisions without real apprehension about the future and had a sense of dread that stayed with me. Going to church did not give me relief because I feel unless you have enough serotonin in your system you are like a car without oil—you cannot really function normally. It may give you solace for a short period but it is a lack of a chemical like not having insulin—your physical body cannot heal itself. You cannot pull yourself up by the boot straps.

—HELEN

I know that I am hypersensitive to criticism about my psychotropic drugs. I easily feel defensive about them. When a famously handsome but not overly bright actor scolded a colleague on national television for using medication to deal with her post-partum depression, I felt a familiar wave of shame, as if he were scolding *me*. But I'm getting better: I also realized immediately that he was a jerk.

I was surprised to learn about fifteen years ago that about ten of the fifteen guys at my AA meeting took antidepressants. Some years later, it was suggested to me that I was probably carrying a burden that could be relieved with minimal medication dosage. I began using Prozac, under medical supervision. I have at no time since then been on cloud nine or enjoyed rose-colored-glasses experiences, but I remember, when I first stopped drinking, how I used to walk down the street from work at night wishing I did not want a drink. Months later, walking down the street, I became aware that for some time I had not experienced that urge and had no idea when it ceased. That relief, I believe, was the result of my working the twelve-step program of AA. I really believe that the medication is also creating a comfort zone, the exact dimension of which may never become apparent to me.

—Tom

Before I started taking medication, I really tried to deal with my depression without medication. All my efforts produced no results. I tried to change my thoughts, but no change lasted more than a few seconds. I tried to stand up for myself, but could not believe in my own worth enough to do so effectively. I prayed to know that God cares for me, and simply could not believe it.

When I started taking medication, the first thing I noticed was that I could think clearly again. I lay awake at night and thought for hours, just for the sheer pleasure of thinking clearly. That happened very soon after starting the antidepressant.

The next thing I noticed was that effort to work on emotional problems actually had results. Instead of being fruitless and pointless, when I made an effort to change my thoughts, it worked. When I spoke up for myself, I felt better instead of like a fraud. When I tried to focus on my own giftedness as a child of God, I found that I could believe that God had in fact created me to be a gift, just like everyone else.

—ADELAIDE

Clarity of thought. The capacity to participate in one's own transformation. The ability to see oneself as both gift and gifted.

Quite simply, the opposite of shame.

CHAPTER 7

THIS IS MY LAST HOPE

Electroshock therapy—one thinks immediately of Boris Karloff, or at least I do: thunder and lightning and terrible darkness outside the tall windows, fearsome arcs of electricity inside, a body jerking once, twice, then arching its back fantastically until it almost falls off the cold metal table on which it lies. Or alternatively, of the electric chair: Old Betsy. A masked and shackled man is strapped into the chair, which resembles a nightmarish throne. The switch is pulled. His gloved fingers begin to smoke. Then his head bursts into flame. *Oh, Jesus*, someone says.

It isn't called electroshock therapy anymore, actually; it's now known as electroconvulsive therapy. In the trade, it goes by a neutral set of initials, ECT. I suppose that sounds kinder—this is a therapy with a lot to live down.

I myself experienced a jolt of electricity to restart my heart, once, but of course I don't remember it: electric shock erases the memory of itself, and often grabs a little more short-term memory on its way out the door. To sign up for electroshock therapy is also to sign over a bit of brain power, which you will never see again. Maybe it hurts, maybe it doesn't—in any case, you don't remember. Still, it's not something a person would do lightly.

And Mary wasn't doing it lightly, not at all. She'd been deeply depressed ever since I'd known her. A gifted musician, she could appreciate beauty and goodness, but she could not summon a joyous response. She had a mordant wit, and could appreciate the wit of others, but her laugh came as if reluctant, creaky as if with disuse, and even her smile was accompanied by a worried brow.

How long has it been this way? I asked.

My whole life, she said, and told me the story of it, a weary tale of passive neglect, related so matter-of-factly, a brief sad telling that ended in a sigh. Not the worst childhood I've ever heard of, I suppose, but far from the best. And so what if it wasn't the worst? Who has the right to compare one child's suffering to another's? As I listened, I had a vision of a little girl's soul quietly starving.

Hours of therapy, of all kinds. Weeks, *months*, probably, if laid end to end, and no improvement. Every time a new medication came out, she experienced a little flurry of hope, but none of them touched it. People would suggest remedies: this or that new therapy, this or that new drug. Even she grew weary of hearing herself answer, *No, I tried that and it didn't work for me,* as if she were somehow letting down the team.

She feared wearing out her welcome. Wouldn't there come a time when people tired of her sadness? When they would no longer admit her to their fellowship because of it? Already she sensed the impatience of those who cared about her.

Most of these were church people. Mary loved the liturgy. She liked it reverent and ordered, replete with incense and ancient chant, with music that was as good as music can get. She loved a good sermon, and she treasured the Eucharist: this bread, this wine was the very Body and Blood of Christ, and it was as broken as she was. She loved all these things. But like all the other things she loved, they did not fill her with joy enough to spill over into the rest of her life. Their absence could hurt her, but their presence did not seem to help. It was the same with the beauty of her singing. She knew it to be beautiful, and treasured the beauty carefully. She was pained when it was less than lovely, but she was never filled with joy, even when she knew it to be well nigh perfect.

Mary does not remember when she first heard about electroshock therapy for depression. It sounded all but fatal, all right, but that didn't seem a particularly powerful argument against it—was there really all that much to lose? Deciding to go forward was not as difficult as a person might imagine.

And people who cared about her wanted her to try it. ECT has changed a lot in the decades since it was introduced, and it has enjoyed remarkable success in cases of depression that resist every other kind of therapeutic approach. It can take someone who can barely move and restore that person to a life with joy in it. So OK, whatever.

A hospital gown and a gurney. A nurse and an anesthesiologist, as well as her doctor. Electrodes attached to her head. *This will not hurt*, she was told, *and you will have no memory of it in any case. A majority of people feel better immediately.*

And Mary was one of them.

Well, how are you? I asked when I visited after the treatment.

I'm great! she said, meaning it. Her smile was radiant.

What do you remember about it? I asked.

Nothing! She laughed, and so did I.

So how many are there whose frozen lives would be transformed by this? How many who could smile radiantly for the first time in years? Maybe ever? How many people are appropriate candidates for electroshock therapy? Lots, probably.

And how many people are likely to volunteer for it? Not very many.

Absolutely not, said a friend. *I would never do that. Didn't you see* One Flew over the Cuckoo's Nest?

I might, if I were in enough pain, said another friend thoughtfully, with a quick glance at me. We share a secret bond: he suffers from depression, too.

Like all the interventions into the neurochemistry of depression, electroshock therapy has learned detractors. *You know, prayer is actually a form of energy,* a friend who is an engineer tells me. Besides being an engineer at a major state university, he is a practitioner of Reiki, the Japanese technique of healing by directing the life force through the hands of the practitioner. Not even hands are necessary, he tells me: he often practices his art from a distance, over the phone, for instance, at an agreed-upon time, when he and his client are in different cities. *It doesn't matter where you are,* he says, *there is no physical distance in spiritual matters. It's right there, right away.*

That being the case, he sees no good reason to shoot voltage directly into the hardware. *Why fry your brain if you already have the means of healing at your fingertips?*

And I wouldn't be too casual about the memory loss, my older daughter said. *You don't get to choose how much short-term memory you'll lose, you know.*

I was curious about how Mary had fared. Ten years have passed since her electroconvulsive therapy. I wanted to know how she's been doing—I have some idea, because she and I have seen each other now and then since that time, and I know she's got a job she enjoys. But we hadn't talked about it since those days. We met for lunch.

She looked beautiful—more deliberately groomed than I remember her being, with lipstick and a sharp outfit. I remember her dressed in drab colors, always, as if trying to blend in with her surroundings. She had just ended a love affair; the Mary I remembered didn't *have* love affairs. This one has had several—certainly, this was a change. I tried to hide the fact that I was aflame with curiosity: was Mary one of the miracle people whose depression disappeared forever after electroshock therapy?

We talked of parishioners and friends, people we both knew, work, musicians, music. *So what is Holy Week like for you now?* I asked her after a time. We had served together for several years in a church whose Holy Week liturgies were especially beautiful. I remembered her, present long after her singing duties were done, keeping the long watch on Maundy Thursday and into the wee hours of Good Friday. The liturgies of Holy Week create their own world, one in which the full range of human sorrow is on display. They walk us through everything: personal failure, tedium and exhaustion, the betrayal of friends, physical pain, the desolation of loneliness and abandonment, the crush of disappointed hope, the finality of death.

I have walked this walk and been stirred by it for many years. No priest is ever anything but weary by the time Holy Week comes around: Lent was long and strenuous, with extra services to lead, extra classes to teach, more confessions than usual, more sermons to prepare. You're tired by the end of Lent. And then it's Holy Week.

My own worst times have settled into the contours of Holy Week with a dreadful ease, as if the liturgies were metaphors for my own pain. And they are, of course: there is no sorrow foreign to a God who has chosen to become human and died for it. Keenly aware of my privilege relative to almost everybody else in the world—housed, fed, free to move about and able to do so—and of the self-centeredness of my doldrums, I lecture myself sternly about counting my blessings, an enterprise unlikely to produce much in the way of spontaneous gratitude. Holy Week provides a matrix for the sorrowful, a *way in* for those of us whose joy is in short supply.

We needn't try to look happy or smile a lot. The music carries our sadness along with us as we proceed, and for seven days, nobody tries to cheer us up.

But although not having to come up with bundles of good cheer from the bare cupboards of our hearts can be a distinct relief, the intensity of Holy Week is hard. We both do and do *not* want to know our own pain, but Holy Week doesn't take no for an answer. Here is Mary, writing in her journal during Holy Week, at the bottom of her depression:

> For the first time in twenty-five years I am reluctant to begin the Holy Week services. Too much emotion, too much activity. . . . Tomorrow, Palm Sunday, is the overture. Holy Week begins. We begin our journey as we recall Jesus beginning his final journey.
>
> I am uneasy. The experience is powerful, and right now I don't know if I have the capacity to bear it. The depth of these experiences feels to me like a very loud sound, from which I shrink. Too much sorrow, too much love. . . . Love and Sorrow are inseparable. No matter how bare the church is, it is filled with Love. No matter how barren, how desolate your heart, Love is there. There is no place where Love cannot go.

But there are plenty of places *we* don't want to go. We want the splint of our numbness to protect us from feeling what we know is there.

During the night on Thursday, a watch is kept before the consecrated bread, the presence of Christ, his body for us. . . . Can't you watch with me even one hour? asked Jesus. So now we take turns, each to pray for an hour in the night before the sacrament. I love doing it, and sign up for 3 A.M. In the silence of the night, in a darkened church, in a small circle of dim light from a few candles, with no distractions, I have had some of my best conversations with God. There is a suggested series of meditations I use, taking account of my life, dropping the barriers between me and God, being honest before him and admitting my need of him.

In the darkness I suddenly have a fantasy that it is my body in the tabernacle, and God is the one keeping watch, waiting for my resurrection.

—MARY

Reading Mary's thoughts reminds me of my own, of how aware I always am of the great beauty and great love in the liturgy, of how many miles distant I can be from it at the very same time.

I sing lines that seem very distant to me. "O Lord my God, I cried out to you, and you restored me to health. . . . You restored my life as I was going down to the grave." I do not feel this, and must sing it on faith; in the hope that one day I will feel this way. If God could do it for a valley full of dry bones, why not for me?

—MARY

Holy Week has never again been as intense for Mary as it was in those dark days. Interestingly, she does not view that fact as related to her depression, but to other factors external to herself—an unwelcome change in choirmasters, and a brief stint singing at another church where the liturgy was nowhere near as lovely.

Mary left the hospital before having another ECT treatment and never went back. Ordinarily, people have about ten treatments over a period of six months or so. Sometimes more. *Everyone who knew me then says that I am better now*, she told me. *People said I made a miraculous change after the treatment. I didn't really see it myself. Not that I remember.*

I certainly saw it. But what to make of her decision not to follow it up with more treatments? And what to make of her dazzling smile in the hospital? I believe that she is telling the truth as she remembers it now. Of course. But I remember that smile.

I did whatever I had to do to make them let me out of there, she said.

Oh.

But Mary does know that she is better—only this is not because her depression has lifted. As far as she is concerned, it has *not* lifted. But she has come to view it differently. She now realizes that it is cyclical, that it ebbs and flows in its severity. *When it's bad, I know that a time will come when it isn't as bad. I know what it is. I've stopped trying and trying to find a cure for it. It's just a part of who I am.*

Hmm. She sounded much less like a victim than she used to sound. Who knows—maybe her single ECT treatment raised all the boats just a little. Or maybe not. Maybe Mary just learned to see things in a different way.

That's the thing—depression is hard to hold in your hand, hard to describe and hard to delineate. There are so many different kinds of depression, with so many different symptoms. And there are so many ideological molds into which individual experiences of depression are poured—our experiences are never uncoupled from our interpretations of them. And no two sufferers are ever the same. It's never clear how it begins or ends—you just *notice* it, after it has already happened.

In the best moments, Holy Week for me is still as I described it. . . . Perhaps with less despair. But the process of becoming empty, to feel the cleansing, prophetic wind sweeping through my soul, to be filled with music containing joy and sorrow and love in a single note—that is still the same. . . .

I used to think that being happy meant that God was with me, and being unhappy meant that God was not with me. I assumed that my depression meant that God had

abandoned me, because if God were with me, I would feel
happy. It laid an extra layer of distress on me, as I felt guilty
for being depressed, as if my feelings had caused God to
leave. As if it were up to me to control God, making him be
with me, or not, by what I felt. Of course it also painted an
unflattering picture of a God who only wants to be around
shiny happy people. And if I felt abandoned, it was my own
fault, for not being shiny and happy.

Contemplative spirituality taught me that the Holy
One is never absent. He is, however, silent. Eventually I
learned that while I may want a God who hugs me, who
protects me from pain, who delivers what I need at any
given moment, what I get is a silent God who turns things
upside down, transforms pain, and can redeem even the
worst situations. God is not going to fix my depression. But
he didn't cause it, either. And he stays with me through
it, loving me anyway. I have learned that even when I feel
empty, even when I can't sense it, Love is there. And it's not
up to me. He is there no matter what I do or how I feel.

—MARY

ELECTRIC POEM

To come home after nights without power
to batteries rolling about exhausted,
computer candlelit and TV staring,
is to know that what makes a home
is electricity, being able to whisper "I'm back"
to the suppressed excitement of cables
everywhere buried alive, ready to burst into
light and music, and oven smells, and print.

Tonight you can give the power station turbine
an extra turn in appreciation of the copper-headed,
moonlighting electrician you were lucky to find,
who can shock Perspex logs into life,
walk between ceiling joists while peeling a cable,
unfold himself limb by limb from the cupboard
(only the wiry win through) and switch from alpha
to beta the rhythms that jolt the heart.

An electrician is trained to hide things
under and over, behind and inside whatever,
and says that when he's gone you'll need

(*Continued*)

an electrometer to know where he's been.
And of course the Creator was an electrician
with elementary particles in his care,
not a carpenter. And certainly not a plumber.

    —SAM GARDINER[1]

CHAPTER 8

SORROWFUL MYSTERIES

A man in the Port Authority approached me with a Bible in one hand and a stack of cards in the other. *Good morning, Sister,* he said, and handed me one of the cards. I was hurrying for the shuttle to Grand Central, though, so I stuffed it in my purse without looking at it. I forgot all about it until it was time to rummage for my ticket to Westchester and there it was.

Do not end up like Mother Teresa! it said, and there was a picture of her in the familiar habit of her Missionaries of Charity. She looked terrible, thin and anxious, a wraith; she looked like the Spirit of Christmas Past. *Come Be My Light,* a collection of her private letters, had just been published, and it had made a bit of a splash. Much of what the letters revealed was not a surprise: the story of her determination to begin a new religious order in the slums of Calcutta, her selflessness, her great humility. But the tabloids had fastened on the startling fact that the Saint of Calcutta had had no personal experience of the love of God for the last forty years of her life. Her private sorrow was splashed across their pages as if she had been caught *in flagrante*. The implication was that she was a hypocrite. This was certainly the belief of militant atheist Christopher Hitchens, the most erudite of Mother Teresa's detractors: "The Church should have had the elementary decency to let the earth lie lightly on this troubled and miserable lady, and not to invoke her long anguish to recruit the credulous to a blind faith in which she herself long ceased to believe."[1]

One thinks of most hypocrites, though, as being a bit more jubilant about their successful scams than Mother Teresa seems to have been about her life.

> I just long and long for God—and then it is that I feel—He does not want me—He is not there—God does not want me—
>
> Please pray for me that I may not spoil His work and that Our Lord may show himself—for there is such terrible darkness within me, as if everything was dead. It has been like this more or less from the time I started "the work" [Mother Teresa's term for the founding of her Missionaries of Charity]. . . .
>
> Please pray for me, that it may please God to lift this darkness from my soul for only a few days. For sometimes

the agony of desolation is so great and at the same time the
longing for the Absent One so deep, that the only prayer
which I can still say is—Sacred Heart of Jesus I trust in
thee—I will satiate Thy thirst for souls.[2]

The rest of the card the man in the Port Authority
handed me made it clear that it was, in fact, advertising
another book—his own—and that it was an anti-Catholic
treatise. Mother Teresa's main problem was that she was
Catholic. What would have helped, I discovered upon
visiting his Web site, would have been for Mother Teresa to
become a member of *his* church instead. Her inner sorrow
seemed proof to him that she was on the wrong theological
track. As he put it, Mother Teresa "did not know God."

As I rode the train and read the card, I leapt to her
defense. The woman gives up everything sweet and easy
in life to live and work among the poor for forty years and
more, and we condemn her because she doesn't *feel* the
way we imagine she should? Who says that being a person
of faith means you can never be sad? Never be sick at heart?
As always, I had a hidden agenda: Mother Teresa and I, it
seemed, had something in common. The crudely designed
card in my hand disparaged her, and I felt disparaged.

The letters in *Come Be My Light* went back decades.
There were excerpts of letters from the earliest years of
Mother Teresa's vocation, in which she wrote excitedly

of herself as Jesus' "little spouse," as giddy with happiness
as any new bride. But the intimacy of her walk with God
dried up as she went further in her vocation, and vanished
altogether as her work of service in the Calcutta slums
was established and grew. As she grew more and more
famous—lauded as a living saint, consulted as an oracle, an
icon of compassionate service revered by popes and presi-
dents the world over—her inner life grew steadily lonelier.
Sometimes she would just sit with her spiritual director in
silence, unable to speak at all.

She struggled to understand. She wrote to confessor
after confessor of her great interior darkness, her constant thirst for the presence of God and God's equally
constant absence.

At first, her interpretation of her plight was that of
my friend in the Port Authority: she must be on the wrong
track. Mother Teresa was part of a dutiful generation, one
that hoped for a fairly immediate relationship between
right behavior and a reasonable happiness, and expected to
locate the source of most affliction somewhere within the
behavior of the sufferer. Did her inner desolation mean that
she was trying to do the wrong thing at the wrong time in
the wrong place? Was she failing to follow the divine will?

In the spirit of holy obedience, she trusted the authority
of her spiritual directors—she would give up the work in a

moment, she said repeatedly, if they directed her to do so. And she trusted the indelible early experiences of her calling, experiences which had been full in equal measure of the palpable sense of both God's love and God's demand. She remembered that these had indeed *happened*, that they had been as real as anything else in the universe, too real to deny. She remembered the moment at which her calling to go into the slums and serve the poorest of the poor occurred: it was on September 10, 1946, while she rode the train from Calcutta to Darjeeling. It is still celebrated by the Missionaries of Charity as "Inspiration Day." "It was on this day in 1946 in the train to Darjeeling that God gave me the 'call within a call' [that is, a call to further specific service; Mother Teresa was already a Loreto nun at that time] to satiate the thirst of Jesus by serving Him in the poorest of the poor."[3]

Jesus had asked her to satiate what she called his "thirst for souls" by carrying him into the slums in which the poorest of the Indian poor lived: *Come, come, carry Me into the holes of the poor. Come, be my light.*[4] The rest of the train ride had been an extended and dreamlike mystical conversation between Mother Teresa and Jesus: *Wilt thou refuse?* he had asked her, a question she never forgot, one with which she challenged herself for the remainder of her life. *Wilt thou refuse?* he had asked. It had been as plain as day.

No, she would not refuse. And she never did. Her subsequent struggle to bring her response to this call into being
was a hard one. A nun lives under a vow of obedience, and
this new work would require permission from religious supe-
riors, bishops, and, ultimately, from the Pope himself. There
were frustrating exchanges of letters, months of waiting for
each answer, years of answering powerful people's doubts
about the validity of the call, about its feasibility, hard questions about her own motives in taking it up. In spiritual
direction she explained and re-explained the call, gradually
convincing the men who would assist the hierarchy in eval-
uating it that it was a true one. Nobody was more suspicious
of her own ego than Mother Teresa herself: her fear of her
own aggrandizement bordered on panic: "Pray for light that
I may see and courage to do away with anything of self in the
work. I must disappear completely—if I want God to have
the whole."[5] Once the work in the slums began, the sisters'
work was herculean. Mother Teresa persevered in spiritual
direction with several priests and bishops, often finding it
difficult to travel to them. The spiritual aridity within her
took root in this period of her life, at the very time when she
was actually beginning the task to which she had devoted
so much planning and prayer, and it never lifted. Her darkness did not stop her: doggedly, she continued building her
order and expanding their work among the poorest of the

poor; over the remaining four decades of her life and the ten years since then, the Missionary Sisters of Charity grew from thirteen sisters in Calcutta in 1952 to more than 4,500 serving 517 missions in 133 countries worldwide today. In 1979, Mother Teresa won the Nobel Peace prize. But she died in 1998, never again having felt the delight of God's presence that had animated her as a young nun.

Gradually, she came to believe that her interior darkness was part of her vocation, an almost compensatory substituting project of giving her own joy away that Christ's joy might be increased. "Pray for me," she wrote, "for everything within me is icy cold. It is only that blind faith that carries me through for in reality to me all is darkness. As long as Our Lord has all the pleasure—I really do not count."[6]

She regarded it as a curious sort of gift to other people; she endured darkness in order that they might enjoy light: "If I ever become a saint, it will surely be one of 'darkness.' I will continually be absent from Heaven—to light the light of those in darkness on earth."[7]

I don't think "depression" was part of Mother Teresa's vocabulary: her generation in the religious life regarded feelings as a luxury at best and a considerable danger at worst. Above all else, they sought to be creatures of will, and then strove to subordinate that will to the divine will. The idea that a disease of her brain's chemistry—exacerbated, surely, by simple exhaustion—might have something to do with her brokenness would have seemed to her an unworthy refusal to accept responsibility for herself.

What would we prescribe for Mother Teresa, we armchair psychologists who didn't know her? Probably that she ought to ease up on herself. And get some professional help. We probably wouldn't have recommended the doggedness with which she persevered, both in her work and in her unrequited prayer for God's presence. Of course, if she'd taken *our* advice, she would not have accomplished all she did. At conferences about wellness, in our therapists' offices, we assure each other confidently that only a balanced life produces good fruit. But nobody could call Mother Teresa's life balanced, and it produced a lot. Hmm.

I often took Mother Teresa as an example for myself as a parish priest. If this tiny woman could push and push herself, could accomplish so much, I'd say to myself when I was tired, then surely so could I. She lives in *Calcutta*, for heaven's sake—I'm in New York City, where clean water flows from every tap, where there is much more than enough of everything.

I remember reading in a magazine about an American who, on a visit to Calcutta, requested to meet her. Might he call on her? No, she said, I'll come to you, and at precisely the agreed-upon time, the famous little figure in her white sari appeared at his door. Such humility, I thought. *I* should be like that. I should go to the people who want to see me, like Mother Teresa.

In those days, I didn't know about her spiritual starvation—like everybody except Christopher Hitchens, I assumed that a rich lode of God's presence fed her constantly, fueling her tremendous output of work. Now I read through her letters and see that she was more like me than I imagined, that she knew emptiness, as I know emptiness. Now I see that I *am* like Mother Teresa, only not in the way I wanted to be like her. I won't become a living saint, like she did. If I am like her, it will be in my brokenness, not in my achievement.

The umbrage we take at depression in people of faith lies in a mistaken idea of what faith is for: we imagine that a closer walk with God will make us consistently happy. We're so committed to this idea that some of us take sorrow on the part of religious people as evidence of their hypocrisy. Here is Christopher Hitchens again: "She was no more exempt from the realization that religion is a human fabrication than any other person, and that her attempted cure was more and more professions of faith could only have deepened the pit that she had dug for herself."[8]

Well, *of course* Hitchens thinks that: he has no use for any religious leader. But why a *Christian* would equate the

presence of pain with absence of faith I don't know, since so
many of us wear little crosses—the first century equivalent
of electric chairs—around our necks. Still, many of us persist in this belief, and it is not so. Neither faith nor the lack
of it guarantees happiness. No one is happy all the time. We
have moods. They come with our humanity.

There is no doubt that Mother Teresa did conceal her
true condition from her sisters and from an adoring world.
Like so many of us, she hid her sorrow behind a smile.
This was a triumph of her considerable will over her painful emotions, and it was one she recommended to anyone
else so afflicted. Mother Teresa recommended a big smile,
always: "The darkness is so dark and the pain so great, but in
spite of it all—my retreat resolution was the same: A hearty
"Yes" to God, a big "Smile" to all. And it seems to me that
these two words are the only thing that keeps me going. . . .
Pray for me, Father, that I may just keep the two words "Yes"
and "Smile."[9]

It would cover whatever weariness or impatience, whatever jealousy or anger, whatever doubt lay beneath it. A big
smile would change the world.

Nobody but her spiritual directors knew about the dark
part of her life: "Father, I do realize that when I open my
mouth to speak to the sisters and to people about God and
God's work it brings them light, joy and courage. But I get

nothing of it. Inside it is all dark and feeling that I am totally cut off from God."[10]

Certainly, she wanted to keep her desolation hidden. She felt it best, in fact, that she disappear entirely from the record of her work. Always uncomfortable with the adulation she attracted wherever she went, she begged everyone who wrote about her to write about the work instead, not about her, to ascribe it all to Christ, not to her.

> I want the work to remain only His. When the beginning will be known people will think more of me—less of Jesus. Please for Our Lady's sake do not tell or give anything. . . .
>
> I am afraid we are getting too much publicity. A few things I heard this evening have made me feel cold with fear. God preserve us. Please pray for me—that I be nothing to the world and let the world be nothing to me.[11]

Mother Teresa was suspicious of her own personal power and of its spiritual allure. She remembered her girlhood self as arrogant:

> I want to be only all for Jesus. . . . Many times this goes upside down—so my most reverend "I" gets the most important place. Always the same proud Gonxha [her Albanian name].
>
> I am longing—with a painful longing to be all for God—to be holy in such a way that Jesus can live His life

to the full in me. The more I want Him—the less I am
wanted—I want to love Him as He has not been loved—and
yet there is that separation—that terrible emptiness, that
feeling of absence from God.[12]

Ah, the poor child! That poor saint of the very poor!
So alone, and so desolate at being so alone! At last, she
concluded that her suffering was a gift to Jesus himself,
that her own pain was consecrated to the increase of his
joy. Better this grotesque form of meaning—a God who
demanded her spiritual barrenness as the price of his own
joy—than to explore the possibility that the barrenness itself
might be a symptom of an illness. It doesn't seem that the
idea that she might be suffering from depression was ever
presented to Mother Teresa as a possibility, nor does it seem
that those who, since her death, have studied and written
about her life in support of her canonization have explored
it. Perhaps they share the same suspicion of the idea of
depression as a disease that so many people of faith—and
so many *other* people—share. The venerable mystical motif
of the Dark Night of the Soul, one that dates back to early
Christian centuries, stood by as a ready descriptor of all her
inner darkness, for her, her spiritual directors, and her biog-
raphers, and no one felt the need to look further.

The editor of her letters thought about Mother Teresa's
bleak inner life in spiritual and moral terms:

My answer to the confession of these pages was simple:
there was no indication of any serious failure on her part
which could explain the spiritual dryness. It was simply
the dark night of which all masters of spiritual life know—
though I never found it so deeply, and for so many years
as in her. There is no human remedy against it. It can be
borne only in the assurance of God's hidden presence and
of the union with Jesus who in His passion had to bear the
burden and darkness of the sinful world for our salvation.
The sure sign of God's hidden presence in this darkness is
the thirst for God, the craving for his light. No one can long
for God unless God is present in his/her heart. Thus the
only response to this trial is the total surrender to God and
the acceptance of the darkness in union with Jesus.[13]

And what if the idea of clinical depression *had* entered
into the long conversations Mother Teresa had with her
spiritual directors? It was the 1940s, the 1950s—what secu-
lar remedies were there for depression then? Inappropriately
prescribed tranquilizers. Talk therapy, which cannot have
been readily available in the city of Calcutta, or anywhere
else in India at the time. Maybe the antique categories of
her own ascetical tradition were the best that was to be had.
In any case, they were the only ones she knew about.

Those, and that big smile.

CHAPTER 9

THE DARK NIGHT

A new religious vocation. A religious conversion, even. Or an adult embrace of a childhood faith, quickening everything about its observance into exciting new life. New life in faith is like being in love. It is easy to establish prayer habits, easy to read deeply in sacred texts and other holy writings. The hunger is constant, the rewards many and exceedingly sweet. You can't get enough of God.

It doesn't last, not at that pitch. New love cannot remain new; it must age. This need not be experienced as a loss. By its nature, human love mellows, grafts itself permanently onto the heart—all human love, love of God or love of anything else. Human love changes; that's part of what makes it human. In many people, it can change imperceptibly, gently.

Not always, though. Sometimes it changes abruptly, alarmingly. Sometimes it seems as if the love has gone, as if God has gone away, as if the life has been sucked out of prayer and everything connected with it. Practices that used to bring delight bring nothing but boredom, impatience, and guilty confusion about feeling these things. And a terrible sense of bereavement: *They have taken away my Lord,* your stricken soul wails, *and I do not know where they have laid him.*

Besides normal sorrow and abnormal depression, there is another darkness: what the mystics have long called the Dark Night of the Soul. The Dark Night may or may not happen in the midst of either sorrow or depression—or both—but it is not the same thing as either of these. If sorrow is about loss, and depression is about bitter despair, the Dark Night is about mystery—its obscurity cloaks all meaning, so that none of it is clearly visible. You can't find your familiar landmarks. There was a time in your life, you remember, when prayer was a delight, an intimate conversation that sustained you throughout the day. No more. Now, the prayers that used to sustain you are about as inspiring as brushing your teeth. You sit numbly before the blank page of the journal you have enjoyed keeping for years, and nothing comes to your pen. God seems far away and silent; the evidence of the divine presence in your life and practice fails to rise above the level of hearsay—you sense nothing of it yourself. *What is God doing? Where is God? Who am I? What on earth is happening to me?* You long for faith to come alive again; you try every spiritual practice you can think of. You try new ones. But none of them seems able to overcome the silence and strangeness that have settled on your heart.

As confusing and even frightening as it can be, the Dark Night is a growing season in a person's spiritual journey. It is recognized as such only after it is over. It is reported—though not always so named—by almost every spiritual guide who has ever written a memoir. A time of challenge and uncertainty, perhaps of great pain or perhaps not: the one enduring the Dark Night of the Soul is in eminent company. Here is John of the Cross, the sixteenth-century Spanish monk who coined the phrase:

> One dark night,
> fired with love's urgent longings
> —ah, the sheer grace!—
> I went out unseen,
> my house being now all stilled.

In this first stanza, the soul speaks of the way it followed in its departure from love of both self and

all things. Through a method of true mortification, it
died to all these things and to itself. It did this so as to
reach the sweet and delightful life of love with God.
And it declares that this departure was a dark night. . . .
This dark night signifies here purgative contemplation,
which passively causes in the soul this negation of self.[1]

And here is his friend and mentor, the more briskly practical Teresa of Avila, addressing her creator: "If this be the way
you treat your friends, no wonder you have so few of them."[2]

It makes every bit of sense for a person to whom faith is
a matter of importance—even one who doesn't think that
all human sorrow can be magically prayed out the window—to hope that it will somehow illuminate the darkness
of depression. We understand that nobody ever promised us
a rose garden, but could we perhaps have a little light? Of
course we redouble our prayer in the hard times—prayer
has nourished us in the past, and we want that nourish-
ment again. But our mind-misery is immovable, unable to
appeal to a court higher than that of our own hopelessness.
It might not be too much to say that a depressed person of
faith almost always experiences a dark night of the soul as
well, whatever means of healing he or she eventually finds:
that the hopelessness is the illness, and the mystery whose
shape gradually emerges as dawn breaks is the dark night,
the eventual blessing of meaning's return.

During the more ordinary course of my depression, before my
hospitalization, I had two distinct spiritual periods. During
one period, I prayed often, but not in a way that brought
any peace or relief. My prayer life felt as flat as the rest of
my emotional life. I would ask for strength to keep doing my
duty, but my imagination did not get big enough to ask for
healing for my depression or to guide me in that direction.

During a later period, I was furious with God (largely
over ongoing infertility) and not really on speaking terms.
All I wanted when I thought about faith was to be in the
church alone so I could holler at the altar, and I stopped
going to church because every week seemed to be another
reading about barrenness or miracle babies or both. It's the
only extended period in my life (about a year and a half) of
withdrawal from God and from prayer.

The two big parts of my recovery have been medication
with therapy, and regular daily prayer time. After my
hospitalization was over, as I grew stronger, I found that
I was able to attend church and to pray again. My fury was
gone and my prayer life became more meaningful.

— STEPHANIE

*You mean my depression might really be the Dark
Night of the Soul?* Somehow that sounds a lot better.
More religious, anyway. *Then how do I tell which it is?* An
understandable hope: who wouldn't want to have something Henri Nouwen or Saint Teresa had, rather than the

awful tedium of mere garden-variety self-loathing? But it may
not be as important to delineate the differences among the
three human experiences of spiritual suffering as an orderly
mind might think it is: simple sorrow, clinical depression,
and the dark night can and sometimes do coexist in us,
and there's no particular need to know which is which, not
right away—since the healing response to all of them is the
same response. That response is no snappy list of surefire
remedies. Instead, it is these two simple things:

1. From others, a quiet and respectful presence, a
   willingness to be beside the one who suffers.
2. From you, a gentle, abiding tenderness toward your
   own battered self while it gropes its way towards
   healing and the restoration of meaning and love.

The late psychiatrist and mystic Gerald May drew a
distinction between the ancient concept of the Dark Night
of the Soul and clinical depression. Both are dark with
uncertainty, apparently rudderless. Both are dry, with no
sense of being accompanied by God. The Dark Night, however, continues to make use of the spiritual tools that were
lively and true before it befell, even though they seem not
to "work" anymore. It struggles to do so. The Dark Night
knows enough to ache for what it is missing.

Depression can't do that. It is not attracted by God or much of anything else. It doubts its own memory of the days when heaven and earth mattered. It wonders if faith was ever real, and then it shrugs its shoulders indifferently at the question. *Like I care*, it sneers. The cartoonish indifference is all an act, of course: tears stand in its eyes.

The thing about the Dark Night and clinical depression is that they often visit side by side. Their resemblance to each other is more than superficial. People of faith may suffer for years from a bitterness which could be eased considerably with medication or talk therapy or both. And it may also be that some people in professional treatment to rid themselves of the modern equivalent of a demon miss the inner spiritual work that might be going on beneath their anguish, simply because the categories presented to them for understanding and healing the psyche are strictly confined to the psychotherapeutic or even more strictly, to the psychopharmacological. It doesn't have to be this way. There is no reason one must choose between God and therapeutic intervention.

> I lived with a fearful case of panic/anxiety disorder after taking care of my very ill and elderly parents for the last fifteen years of their lives. When they died six weeks apart, I was devastated. What I had to hang on to was my innate

belief that God, my Father, was always going to be there and always had been there to care for me and lift me through whatever I had to endure. That, plus a sudden blast of terrific British humor via *Are You Being Served* viewed quite unexpectedly one day after they had died was what it took to begin my healing. It was the laughter that helped. I also was told by a grief counselor that I should take whatever time necessary to heal from this double bereavement, however long or short that might be. The third thing was to be able to talk to the psychiatrist who not only put me on the necessary medication to help replace the serotonin in my brain which was quite depleted due to stress but he listened to me every week for at least two hours for three years. Underneath it all, however, were the everlasting arms and love of God and my husband and close friends. . . . I might also add that talking to God was very important because I knew that He would listen to whatever I had to say and not think it was silly.

—EDNA

INFERNO, CANTO I

Midway upon the journey of our life
I found myself within a forest dark
The straightforward pathway had been lost.
Ah me! How hard a thing it is to say
What was this forest savage, rough and stern,
Which in the very thought renews the fear.
So bitter is it, death is little more;
But of the good to treat, which there I found,
Speak will I of the other things I saw there.
I cannot well repeat how there I entered
So full was I of slumber at the moment
In which I had abandoned the true way.
But after I had reached a mountain's foot
At that point where the valley terminated
Which had with consternation pierced my heart
Upward I looked, and I beheld its shoulders,
Vested already with that planet's rays
Which leadeth others right by every road.
Then was the fear a little quieted
That in my heart's lake had endured throughout the
night,

(*Continued*)

The night, which I had passed so piteously.
And even as he, who with distressful breath,
Forth issued from the sea upon the shore,
Turns to the water perilous and gazes;
So did my soul, that still was fleeing onward,
Turn itself back to behold the pass
Which never yet a living person left.

    —DANTE ALEGHIERI[3]

CHAPTER 10

WORDS FAIL ME

Just pray, the people who love you tell you. *Ask God to help you.* And you try. But the snide voice that lives inside you reminds you that you don't really believe any of this crap, that you're a hypocrite pretending to a faith you do not possess, that you're just trying to look holy. *No, I'm not!* you try to argue. *No, I'm not a hypocrite! Not on purpose, anyway.* But every word you try to say in prayer sounds insincere, heard through the cruel filter of this internal conversation, and you give up. Again.

Even talking to another human being is like this for someone who is depressed, never mind talking to God. *Hello,* someone says innocently, and you struggle for a response. *Hi,* you finally croak, and the person goes away.

I felt as though I had to get everything right and then
"report the outcome" to God. There was no sense that He
was with me in the journey. At one point during separation
and divorce I was telling a friend about one fear and
another—where would I live and how would I support
myself. I remember she asked, "Where is your faith?"
I hardly knew how to answer her.

—SALLY

Here is where an altogether different approach to
prayer might help. It might involve dispatching some fairly
sacred cattle along the way, but if this is too much for you,
you can always go back to prayer that doesn't work. It's a free
country, I always say.

Specifically, we must begin by questioning the importance of words in our prayer. We are wedded to them, afraid
of getting them wrong, irrationally afraid that if we pray for
the wrong thing something terrible may happen. Two people
emerge from the hospital room of a gravely ill patient and
walk together down the corridor. *She's so sick*, one says to the
other, when they are out of earshot, *I don't know whether to
pray for her to live or die*. He says this in all seriousness, as
if the wrong prayer words on his part might push someone
into the hereafter who wasn't going there anyway. We pray
as if it were all up to us, when in fact, almost none of it *is*.

We pray as if we were giving God treatment plans to follow, as if nothing could possibly work out well if we weren't there to plan it. We imagine that we must "know what to pray for" in advance, and that we cannot pray if we don't. That if we cannot "name it and claim it," our prayer will be to no avail.

Oh, come *on*. How likely is this, really? Is God's great goodness really likely to be hostage to our magic words, granted to those who know the code and withheld from those who do not?

Often we do *not* know what should happen in a given situation. And sometimes we know that the things we long for cannot be—we know that nobody lives forever, for instance, and that most people in this world who have died have had at least one person praying mightily that they wouldn't. We cannot look at prayer with an open mind and not conclude that, whatever else it may be, it isn't like placing an order at a pizza parlor.

> It was amazing how hard it was to pray through that time, and still can be. I did it ferociously but felt like it was all my fault. . . . I tried but just couldn't do it. And the guilt from that only tore me up so much more. I actually felt guilty for not being closer to Him—almost in a way that I felt I didn't deserve His love.
> —Netta

Maybe we could lean instead into a form of prayer that takes seriously what we say we believe: that God is in and around all of human history, absent from none of it. God is not a figure outside of our experience and in need of information about it. We don't really need to pray *about* anything; we're not in charge of much of what happens in the world. We can content ourselves with prayer from within it all.

So if prayer's efficacy is not measured by whether or not we get what we ask for, it's probably safe to stop asking for things, especially if doing so seems to feed the desperation and despair that take root in the soul of a depressed person—if prayer has become little more than worry with an "Amen" tacked on at the end. Here is a suggestion:

Maybe we could try not using words at all.

Never is this permission to be wordless more important than when depression strangles even the everyday words of human interaction. At such a time, a spiritual practice may be needed that will *allow* your emptiness, rather than fight to fill it. The ancient practice of centering prayer is one, like other meditative techniques from other religions and cultures: the quiet, gentle abdication of all one's illusions of personal power and control. It is not measured by the quality or quantity of emotion it produces. Prayer doesn't have to be measured by anything.

Maybe it won't work, you think sadly. After all, nothing *does*, not for me. But think for a moment: what will happen if you are unable to pray in this quiet way?

I'll be miserable about it.

And aren't you miserable already?

Yes.

So give it a try, then. It seems you have nothing left to lose.

Give yourself twenty minutes or so, at a time and place in which you'll be left alone. You don't want to be checking your watch all the time—you might consider setting a timer, so you don't obsess about how many minutes it's been. But don't make it one of those kitchen timers that would wake the dead—set the timer on your cell phone to a gentle ring tone.

There are four parts to this silent prayer, added one at a time:

1. Marking the breath
2. Sequential relaxation of all parts of the body
3. Introduction of the holy word
4. The descent

Sit in a chair, or on the floor if you prefer. Best not to do this lying down: centering prayer is deeply calming, and you might fall asleep. Not that this would be a terrible thing, mind you—it would just mean that you were tired. Place both feet on the floor and your hands comfortably in your lap. If your shoes or your belt or your eyeglasses bother you, remove them.

1. MARKING THE BREATH

Begin to be aware of your breathing. In and out it goes, so many times a day, for all these years—it is so faithful. The breath is a gift from God, one which has sustained your life ever since you were born. You remember having read somewhere that the Hebrew word for *breath* or *wind* is the same as the one for *spirit*: it is *ruach*. You say it with a soft "k" sound on the end of it, like gently clearing your throat: *Rua-khh. Rua-khh.* It even *sounds* like a breath. In some important way, the Spirit and the breath are the same. The breath is the gift of life.

Throughout this time of prayer, you will continue to notice the breath, to mark it. In and out, deep but not hard. The gift of God, sustaining your life. *Ruach.*

If your mind begins to wander, or if a noise or sensation catches your attention, don't worry about it. Above all, don't try to banish it from your thoughts—that's a sure way to obsess about it. A wandering mind isn't a sign that something's wrong—*everybody* who prays has a wandering mind. Just focus on the breath, in and out, and be patient. It will pass.

2. SEQUENTIAL RELAXATION OF ALL PARTS OF THE BODY

Relaxing your body one part at a time works better than just telling your body to relax: most of us are unaware of our tight muscles, and unable to release them just by ordering ourselves to do so. Tightening a muscle and then releasing it, on the other hand, helps you to see the difference between the two, and seems to "disappear" that part of you from the anxious radar of your concern. Which, after all, is what you're trying to do here: wean your consciousness from its busy management of your body.

Begin with your feet. Tighten them—hard. Point your toes toward the floor as hard as you can. Then flex the feet, hard, pointing your toes toward the ceiling. Hold it—tight tight tight—and then let go. Just let them fall. As soon as you have done this, it will be as if your feet have disappeared. You need have no concern for them. And, all the while, you continue to mark the breath, in and out, deep but not hard. The gift of God.

Turn your attention to the calves of your legs. Again, tighten those muscles and hold—tight tight tight, as hard as you can—and then let go. Now your legs seem to have disappeared below the knee. And all the while you mark the breath, in and out.

Turn your attention to the great muscles of your thighs. Tighten the hamstrings first, on the underside of your thighs—tight tight tight—as hard as you can, hold them—and then let them go. Then tighten your quadriceps, the large muscles in front—tight tight tight—and let them go. Now it seems that your legs are gone altogether. And still, you mark your breath, in and out, deep but not hard. The gift of God.

Proceed in this manner, piece by piece—the muscles of the buttocks, tightening them until they almost lift you off your chair, and then releasing them. Now your abdominal muscles, distending your abdomen and then sucking it in. Hold it tight tight tight—and then release it. Turn your attention to your arms—splay out your fingers as wide as you can, then make a fist as tight as you can—tight tight tight—and then let go. Tighten your biceps, your triceps—tight tight tight—and let them go. Your shoulders—up, up toward your ears, then down, down toward the floor. Push them forward, hard as you can, and then back, hard as you can, opening out your chest, and then let them go. Now tighten your neck muscles, the muscles of your face, your eyebrows, open your mouth as wide as you can—tight tight tight—and then let go. And as always, mark your breath steadily; *notice* it: in and out, in and out.

Now your body is completely soft and relaxed. It is as if it had disappeared. You need have no concern for it. If any part of your body feels uncomfortable or seems to grab for your attention, simply tighten and release it, marking the breath as you do so.

Now it is time for the holy word.

3. INTRODUCTION OF THE HOLY WORD

Your holy word is yours. You choose it. Its function is to carry away your busy thoughts and to carry your spirit into that quiet place that *is* the prayer for which you have come.

What word should you choose? People often want to choose a word that is especially meaningful to them— *Jesus*, perhaps, or *love*, or *forgive*. This is understandable: those are all wonderful words. But remember what the holy word is *for*—it is not chosen primarily for its meaning. Centering prayer is not *about* thought and meaning. In fact, choosing an especially meaningful word may end up distracting you, encouraging you to explore its significance in your mind and giving rise to further thought, when what you are hoping for is the stripping *away* of thought, not its increase. This is why, in Hindu meditation, a non-sense word is chosen, a word like *Om*, one that will not conjure pictures in your mind. Consider instead choosing a holy word that does *not* produce a flood of visual images in your mind—a more abstract word like *holy*, say. Or *sanctus*. Or *glory*.

It's best to choose a word and stick with it. If you discover that the one you've chosen is distressing in some way, or gives rise to too much thought, change it, of course. But part of the holy word's function is to condition your spirit to this form of prayer, and conditioning is all about habit. The word itself takes on the power to guide you, not by its meaning but by the simple repetition of it. If you are constantly changing your Holy Word because you think you need a better one, you lose this opportunity. So relax, and stick with the one you've got.

My own holy word is *Holy God*. I know—that's two words. You're welcome to use it if you like, until you've chosen your own. Or forever. Be my guest.

You begin to repeat the holy word to yourself, over and over again. As you repeat it, it fills your mind, taking up all the space into which a stray idea or distraction might creep. This is its purpose, to help you remain focused for the final stage of this form of prayer. As always, you continue to mark your breath. As you repeat the holy word, they are together in your experience, word and breath in harmony. In a sense, they are one thing.

4. THE DESCENT

You continue to repeat your holy word. If a distraction appears—a noise, a thought, a sensation—simply repeat the holy word until it passes. Sometimes I think of the holy word as being like a toy train—around and around it goes on its circular track, and I can put any noise or thought or sensation that comes up into one of its cars as it passes by. Or I think of it as being like flypaper—my distractions stick to it. Over and over you repeat it, and it collects everything and takes it away.

I think of the descent as being on some kind of circular path. But never is it more important than when attempting to describe this kind of prayer to remember that all religious language is metaphor. So if your imagination takes you to some other image—an ascent, for example, instead of my sense of traveling downward—don't let me stand in your way. For me, in any case, the word repeats and its path spirals downward, down past experience and thought, leaving both behind. Full of the holy word, your mind and spirit become empty of everything else. Your mind becomes like your body, increasingly still. Eventually the holy word itself slips away, leaving stillness in the place where it was.

I can only speak to my own experience of this descent, and any words I come up with are inadequate the moment I've written them. I can say that, for me, the descent includes a distinct sense of being in the presence of a Presence, *within* it, and that this Presence includes me in *its* experience—my organic self, the whole of me, body, mind, and spirit, reduced to a single point. In this place—which is not really a *place* at all—there is no time and the passing of minutes is irrelevant.

I told you it was hard to describe.

Sometime about now, the timer rings. You don't know how long you've been sitting in that chair, and you don't much care. You open your eyes when you're ready. That was centering prayer.

Nothing could be simpler than this experience—it has no moving parts. It has no content, no scripture, no petitions, and no praise. And yet it is prayer at its most basic. When you've finished, you know that much, even if you don't know anything else.

For someone in the paralyzing deadness of depression, when concentration is hard to come by and a bitter voice within ridicules your every attempt to pray, centering prayer may be the way you can enter into the presence of God when nothing else will take you there. Its four steps carry you—*you* don't have to carry a thing. You don't have to struggle resolutely to learn how to "think of nothing"—centering prayer's simple steps do that for you. The wholeness of your yielding to it, bit by bit, *includes* whatever intentions and scattered longings you may have, whatever you think you should be praying about. It's all already *there*, in the simple heart you have brought. Nothing more need be said. God already knows.

Interestingly, in view of the fact that centering prayer is almost completely silent, many find it easier to do it in a group than to do it alone. Why might this be?

Usually, such a group has a leader, who guides the group through the stages of this form of prayer just outlined, and the voice of the leader helps people maintain their focus. And it is also true that a group of people sitting together already *has* something of a communal spirit, a silent but palpable sense of common purpose, such as one experiences in the reading room of a library. For whatever reason, you might find it helpful to look up a centering prayer group—enough people have rediscovered this ancient form of contemplative prayer that an increasing number of parishes have them, as well as convents, monasteries, and theological seminaries. Don't be reluctant to look outside your own denomination; centering prayer is the same wherever you go. You could also form your own group—two or three people are enough to begin. It might be well, though, to work for a while with someone who is experienced in centering prayer, becoming accustomed to it before you strike out on your own.

But is this Christian? It doesn't mention Jesus! Am I not straying from my beliefs by embracing such a thing? You will find no shortage of militant Christian Web sites that warn grimly against any dealings with contemplative spirituality or centering prayer—this one, for example, which calls itself "Lighthouse Trails Research Project: Exposing the Dangers of Contemplative Spirituality": "This very deep-rooted heresy called contemplative spirituality (i.e., spiritual formation) negates the Cross, demeans the sacrifice of Jesus, and nullifies the only way for man to be saved."

My goodness. All that? This is as good a place as any to suggest that God is probably a great deal larger than our fascination with our own confessional purity is willing to countenance. That fascination is a human thing. Many famous mystics have found themselves bored by it: Thomas Merton, for instance, whose *Seven Storey Mountain* has been a spiritual classic since it was published more than sixty years ago, was a Zen Buddhist for many years, as well as a Trappist monk, and experienced no contradiction in being both. Neither did T. S. Eliot understand his deepening interest in Buddhism as being in any way at odds with the Christianity he embraced: his poetry and prose combine a commitment to Christian faith with a deepening conviction that the way of Zen was, in fact, the Way of Jesus. Henri Nouwen was another such person, a priest and teacher of ancient Christian ascetical practice who recognized the Way of Jesus easily, in many different places, in many different faiths and cultures. In general, the more time you spend in Christ's presence, the easier it is for you to recognize him in cultural settings other than the one in which you first encountered him. Like this one, perhaps, in which Christ is not named—the practitioner is not a Christian—but in which the outlines of Christ's healing work are clearly visible to someone who is:

> I struggle with the demons of depression and anxiety, although I no longer give them those names to reside in (because it gives them a "reality" that they thrive upon). Now I work with the concept of "mind-ness." What I mean is that the mind, my mind, is prone to going to the places of suffering, i.e., depression, anxiety, guilt, self-blame, and on and on, as a bad habit. And the awareness of that fact of mind, my mind, gives me the edge, the possibility, of rising above the mechanism and having compassion—compassion for my own self. Oh, my. Just that amount of objectivity between me and my (sometimes crazy, sometimes

brilliant—how to know the difference?) mind gives me
the possibility of rising above the muck of the chronic
"depression/anxiety" vortex.

I guess what I really want to convey is that, having
struggled all my life (I'm sixty-two) with these demons,
and not having succumbed (as my mother did) to their
convincing argument that all is hopelessly f——d, I think that
I have grabbed the tail of hope. Hope not in some idea of
redemption, but in the power of undertaking the journey of
my own self—finding the redemption from inside—I swear
God is in there—and being responsible to and for that.
    —AMANDA

In all such considerations, it is important to remember that spirituality is much more about practice and presence than it is about thinking or speaking, so that propo-
sitional statements about what God is like or what the
Bible says don't really form the basis of it. It need not be
defended or documented in their terms. It need not
be defended at all.

I was afraid you'd be disappointed in me, my friend and
former parishioner said, in explanation of not having told
me before now that she had become a Buddhist. But how
could *I* ever be disappointed in anyone else's true spiritual
journey? Knowing what I knew about her, moreover: that
prayer had often been a struggle for her, that she had fought
crippling depression for years?

> I believe in the message of Jesus, but it seems to me that
> the church doesn't. Christian teachings are demanding and
> maybe mostly impossible, but over the centuries, it seems to
> me almost no one in the institutional church has tried very
> hard. I obsessed about the church literally all my thinking
> life. And it feels good not to have that burden anymore.
> —WINIFRED

Ouch. Guilty as charged, all too often. It sounds to me like the inability to hold on to a purely intentioned person like that is the church's failing, not hers. Whatever faith stance she chooses to make, is it possible that God's love could ever fail her? Never. Then why should mine? Is my commitment to my own faith journey, which has led so squarely to Christ, so precarious that it requires me to reject or suspect other people's commitment to theirs? And do I purport to know the mind of God completely? I hope I have never given *that* impression.

Meditative prayer without words is eminently practical. It is anything but otherworldly. It is not necessary to escape ourselves in order to experience an authentic life of the spirit—we are experiencing that life already and just don't know it. Centering prayer is mostly a matter of getting out of our own way.

No spiritual discipline is for everyone. We're all too different for that to be true. If the words you have been using in prayer work well for you, by all means, stay with them. This chapter has been for the ones for whom that has *not* been true, those for whom prayer has become yet another failed path to peace. Centering prayer could be a way back in.

Or a way in for the very first time.

CHAPTER 11

WANTING TO DIE

In a way, the title of this chapter is not accurate, not exactly. Depressed people who want to kill themselves aren't so much longing for death as just longing for the pain to stop. Their thinking is disordered by their disease; it convinces them that the world would not be seriously inconvenienced by an early exit on their part, and might even be a better place if they were not around.

> I lay on the bed to think for a few minutes before I took the pills. God didn't know I existed. I was severely depressed, felt abandoned, and alone. No one actually loved me. I remember thinking, "There is no one on this entire planet who will truly care if I die." And I wanted to die.
>
> My plan was to take an overdose of my thyroid replacement hormone, which I believed would cause a

heart attack. I brought a glass of water into the bedroom and swallowed three Percocet to relieve the pain of the heart attack. I waited about thirty minutes for the Percocet to start taking effect. Then I took one Synthroid, looked at the bottle and said out loud:"This is the dose for the day. Am I ready to go on with it?" I started swallowing pills, one at a time, and thought, "I'm really doing it."

When I got to twenty-five, I decided that should do it. I slept for about five hours, looked at the clock, and said, "Damn it! I'm still alive." I didn't take anything else, but I didn't go to the hospital until the next day. I still wanted to die.

— ESTELLE

Religious people who consider suicide encounter an immediate obstacle: centuries of church teaching which have held that suicide is a mortal sin. It combines murder with despair, a perfect storm.

For the first time in my life, I was truly suicidal. I *do* believe that life is precious, and the fact that I was contemplating taking my own life scared me!

— LIZA

Dante places suicides in a lower circle of hell than murderers. Many adults can remember a time when a person who committed suicide could not be buried in a church cemetery. Many remember a family hush surrounding the sudden death of a relative.

> There were always family whispers that a paternal uncle committed suicide—something else no one talks about.
>   —RAE ANN

And so, to the pain that makes a person want to end it all in the first place is added this pain: *The only remedy I can see is one that I must not take. If I take this means of escape, God will throw my soul into eternal torment. God will punish me forever for being unable to endure my life anymore.*

Many of the people to whom I spoke, all of whom had histories of one or more serious depressions, had thought of committing suicide during their worst moments. For more than a few, those times seem to have come at a young age:

> I remember my mother saying to me when I said something about suicidal thoughts. She brushed it off by saying, Oh, everybody thinks about that once in a while. You just have to remember that we can't do that because we will go to hell if we do. Pray.
>
>   —LINDA

> I remember the first time I was conscious of being depressed; I was six years old.
>
>   —MARJORIE

Some had fantasized about how they might go about taking their own lives. Some had made actual attempts: serious ones, carefully planned, like the very organized young man who showed me a folder he kept on his desk labeled "The End." Or more impulsive decisions to do something irrevocable:

> I started scaring myself by walking in front of cars in [New York City]. I was almost hit many times! I didn't care about the ramifications.
> —DEBORAH

Many more just thought about it passively, vaguely wishing something fatal would happen to them to take the moral freight of suicide out of their hands:

> I am a Christian, but suicide is always lurking around the corner. I have a wonderful husband and family and the thoughts of them keep me hanging on. . . . A good day is one in which I wake up and my first thought is not "Oh dear God, please let this be the day you take me home."
> —ELAINE

Still, while many religious people do fear a terrible punishment if they were to act on their suicidal impulses, some do not. For some, the presence of God was discernable even in the midst of a pain so terrible that death seemed far preferable to life in that condition:

What God said to me that night was, "You do not have to hide these thoughts from me." I think that was a turning point, really; I knew that however I got out of that pain, God would accept me and love me and embrace me forever. What actions I actually decided on were up to me, and regardless of what they might be, God would not reject me. After that, things didn't mend immediately, but what that voice had said stayed with me. It was the anchor that kept me from being swept away.

—KELLY

Do I think I'll go to hell for suicide? Would I go to hell if I ignored or did not treat my diabetes or high blood pressure or whatever? Heavens no! My God is loving and kind.

—ROSEMARY

The person who considers suicide truly believes it to be the only way out of his pain. It is counterintuitive to those who are not suicidal, but death feels to the sufferer like a measure of freedom in an otherwise imprisoned life, a light at the end of an interminable tunnel. *Maybe I can't get better, but at least I can get out.* Years ago, I succeeded in persuading a suicidal woman to give me the large bottle of barbiturates she had hoarded—there were enough pills in that bottle to kill several people. *Promise me you'll keep them, though,* she said, her voice tight with anxiety and tears. *Promise me you won't throw them away.*

I won't throw them away. I opened my bottom desk drawer and put the bottle inside. *I'll keep them right here in my drawer.* She needed to know that her means of escape was still there. She needed the option of ending her pain. To the suicide, the means of death represents an only hope. With some excellent professional help, the woman went on to recover, a long and hard road lasting years. She never asked me for the bottle of pills. It stayed in my drawer for a long time.

We really do have a choice. We don't have to stay here. We are not trapped. As strange as it may seem to someone who is not suicidal, the fact of having the choice to end life is itself life-giving. Having the choice helps people not choose death—underneath all the pain, the organism wants desperately to survive.

That said, none of us owes another person our collaboration in his or her suicide. The malformed thought that can't see beyond current pain is just that: malformed. While it may be the sufferer's truth, it is not the whole truth. The goal for the one who loves him is to help him stay alive long enough to see more of it. This means that a friend might have to abandon the respectful space of choice. If your friend or relative has just swallowed a lethal dose of drugs and calls to tell you about it, your love for him does not preclude dialing 911. On the contrary, it demands it.

And that action is also a healing one in ways beyond the simple fact of avoiding suicide in that moment. An act of pain and desperation, to be sure, suicide can also be a manipulative act. *I'll show you,* the suicide may be saying silently to someone; *I'll kill me!* People in search of ways to end their pain by ensuring someone else's need to know that suicide attempts will not be rewarded. Yes, you do have a choice as to whether you will live or die. But I also have a choice. I cannot live with you if you hold your own death over me like a sword.

It is a complicated tightrope upon which to walk, for one who loves such a sufferer. Don't try to walk it alone. Get good advice from a mental health professional. Call a member of the clergy who seems to have his or her head on straight. Use what power you have—and you may have more than you think you do—to insist on professional intervention.

The contemplation of suicide is bleakly solitary. Pain blinds the one who seeks a final escape: he may plan elaborately, but he does not fully comprehend the effects his action will have on those he leaves behind, like the successful suicide whose death is described below by a close friend:

> One of my oldest and dearest friends, from elementary school throughout our entire lives, took her own life five years ago this July after a long and undiagnosed depression.

We loved her and her adoring husband and children, as
well as her sister and brother and their families. Looking
back on the last years of her life, after her parents died, I
see the signs but it was so difficult for all who loved her.
I think all who lose a friend to suicide somehow feel like
they "should" have known. But of course it isn't possible.
She planned it well and left notes all over the house with
instructions as what needed to be done, what was at the
cleaners, things to arrive by mail order, etc. Her request was
to be buried by her beloved parents. It has been hard on all
of us who knew and loved her.

    — BRENDA

Ah, me. It seemed to her that her effort in keeping the
dry cleaning organized would make up for what her death
would do to her family.

Was there a hint — or more than a hint, if one knew
where to look — of anger in that final round of housekeep-
ing? Was it *communicative* in some way? Had her life
become a series of errands? And did she resent it, in some
hidden way, hidden even to her? Did she fail to ask for
what she needed — well, clearly she did. It sounds like she
didn't know how. This is a hard avenue of inquiry for those
left behind. But for those willing to explore it, a way out
of the unanswerable guilt a survivor feels might be found.
Even those who elect suicide in the face of terminal

illness, who involve their families fully in calm and loving rituals surrounding a deeply considered decision, do not fully grasp what the total legacy of that decision will be or the dimension of the sacrifice they are requiring of those who love them. And how could they? They should be very aware, though, of what they are asking: however sincerely and tenderly their families may want to support the awesome decision to end a life that has become heavier than they can bear, no matter how wholeheartedly they may endorse the choice, no collaboration in deliberately ending another's life is without cost to those who remain. In death, as in life, there really is no such thing as a free lunch.

Early in my ministry, I visited a bedridden woman in our community hospital a number of times. She was a highly intelligent woman and very beautiful, with finely drawn aquiline features, deep blue eyes, and snow-white hair, gathered elegantly into a chignon at the nape of her neck. She had suffered from multiple sclerosis for decades, since her young adulthood, and had been without sight for most of that time. Her husband was a physician: she had already been stricken with her disease when they met, and he had cared for her with great devotion throughout their long marriage.

They were no longer young when I encountered them. I imagined, as I watched how tender he was with her, that he must have worried about what would happen if he should become unable to care for her. In those days, I was too inexperienced a pastor to help them talk about this during her hospital stay. And then she was discharged.

If he was worried about their future, it was not for long. I had a call from her daughter one morning a few weeks later. Both her parents had died suddenly the night before, she told me in a shaky voice. Her father had killed her mother and then himself.

Oh, my.

I hung up the phone and remembered that lovely lady: her lovely hair, her beautiful sightless eyes, her quick wit. Her tender husband. I imagined the scene—the old doctor preparing his wife's final injection, gently inserting the needle in her fragile arm one last time, watching patiently beside her to see when her breathing stilled, and then preparing a second syringe. How sad it must have been, but how tender.

But that wasn't exactly how it went, I found out later that day. He had prepared only one syringe. He had bludgeoned his wife to death with a hammer. And then he had injected himself.

Oh.

Communicative.

Life together is hard. Too hard, sometimes, for some people. And if we can't find one way out of the pain, sometimes we'll take another.

Suicide is *not* painless, not for anybody. No, God won't send you to hell for it—there's more than enough hell to go around, right here on earth.

But there is still no such thing as a free lunch

TO BE OR NOT TO BE

To be, or not to be: that is the question:
Whether 'tis nobler in the mind to suffer
The slings and arrows of outrageous fortune,
Or to take arms against a sea of troubles,
And by opposing end them? To die: to sleep;
No more; and by a sleep to say we end
The heart-ache and the thousand natural shocks
That flesh is heir to, 'tis a consummation
Devoutly to be wish'd. To die, to sleep;
To sleep: perchance to dream: ay, there's the rub;
For in that sleep of death what dreams may come
When we have shuffled off this mortal coil,
Must give us pause: there's the respect
That makes calamity of so long life;
For who would bear the whips and scorns of time,
The oppressor's wrong, the proud man's contumely,
The pangs of despised love, the law's delay,
The insolence of office and the spurns
That patient merit of the unworthy takes,
When he himself might his quietus make
With a bare bodkin? who would fardels bear,
To grunt and sweat under a weary life,

But that the dread of something after death,
The undiscover'd country from whose bourn
No traveller returns, puzzles the will
And makes us rather bear those ills we have
Than fly to others that we know not of?
Thus conscience does make cowards of us all;
And thus the native hue of resolution
Is sicklied o'er with the pale cast of thought,
And enterprises of great pith and moment
With this regard their currents turn awry,
And lose the name of action.[1]

CHAPTER 12

THE FAMILY DISEASE

Let's get one thing straight: just because someone is a tragic figure does not mean that he or she cannot also be a royal pain in the ass. This may be a mean thing for me to write, but it is true. Living with someone with any mental illness can be hard work, and I can't think of any reason other than a misplaced politeness to pretend that it is not.

I struggle with depression. Not my own, a family member's. When I perceive that she's having a hard time, I offer mostly unwanted suggestions and somehow, I turn a comfortable conversation into an antagonistic one. I have learned to apologize and backtrack, but it is hard for me to see it coming, this twisting of intentions and best wishes into name calling and blame. Perhaps I should just stop trying to fix and love, isn't that what we are supposed to do? Listen more and love. And then let it go?

— PAMELA

Whether or not we live in the same household with them, we "live" with them and it is a struggle. When around them or even when writing or e-mailing them, we feel like we are walking on eggshells, never knowing when something we say or do will send them off. We feel manipulated. We *are* manipulated!

— MARILYN

Life together is hard even if one party is *not* depressed. Whoever wrote that line about people getting married and living happily ever after must have stayed single. No human life is happy all the time; and the sanest person in the world cannot help but be annoying once in a while.

The family is the crucible of everything human. In large measure, for good and for ill, it makes us who we are. All families are composed of imperfect people, most of whom are doing the best they can, though some of them are not. Wherever the seams of their imperfections lie, the people in them are bound together by profound love: profound and, sometimes, desperate. We pour every need and longing we have into the leaky vessels with whom we live. They can't hold it all, of course: people are insufficient as objects of utter dependence, however much they may want to oblige.

When we marry, and again when we have children, we buy into a romantic vision of love's sufficiency. Romantic and woefully inaccurate, but we cling to it anyway: *If I just love him enough, everything will be all right with him. My love can transform anything.*

To which there is only one possible response: *You're kidding, right?*

Your love is *love*, for crying out loud, not *magic*. The love we bear one another doesn't inoculate against all of life's sorrows—truth to tell, it doesn't inoculate against any of them. Love doesn't inevitably produce understanding: I may love you or I may not, but no matter which it is, I still can't read your mind.

At last, we tell ourselves, *I've found someone who will love me unconditionally.* Poppycock. Human beings don't love unconditionally. We attach enough strings to our love to tether a truckload of balloons. Our unmet and unacknowledged needs seep into everything we do. They warp our vision of one another and distort our ability to hear one another clearly.

The romanticism through which we filter all our relationships is hard on them. The powerful myth of the family's omnicompetence resembles the absolutism of our expectations of God: just as we imagine that love conquers all, many religious people also think that true faith inoculates the believer against the pain that, sooner or later, will enter every life. Combine the two: embrace the idea that a God who runs your life like a puppeteer selected your spouse and children for you and you alone, and the ups and downs of life together assume cosmic proportions. It's not just a relationship: now it's a test of faith. And failure within it isn't just sad: now, it's a sin.

Add the wrong tincture of neurotransmitters, and the world becomes a hard place indeed.

> I do not think my husband was depressed when we married.
> It was unknown to me that he had several bouts of depression
> earlier and at least one suicide attempt before we met. It
> was a storybook romance and after all that has happened,
> we are still very much in love. . . . In the beginning I
> couldn't understand what was happening. . . . It didn't take
> long before he spiraled downward and it became clear that
> something major was wrong. . . . There have been years
> of being out of work due to depression, years of sitting and
> staring, another suicide attempt last year, this time with me
> there, struggling with a loaded gun that went off in the house.
> Years of isolation. Years of not sharing this with anyone due
> to the stigma and out of loyalty. Years of guilt if I should find
> pleasure in a bike ride or in a sunset, or a good book.
>   — RENATA

Like religious faith, the family anchors itself in powerful tradition, and seeks to replicate its past experience in subsequent generations. Often—usually—it does this without being fully aware of it. Renata's father had lived with crippling depression throughout the years of her growing up.

> It's funny that the one thing that I did not want to do was
> to become like my mother and yet . . . here I was. It took a
> while to see it, probably it was too painful to admit at first,
> but it became pretty obvious after T.'s depression took hold.
> It was all so familiar, the hating holidays, the long periods
> of silence, the anger, the isolation, the control. My mother
> would call me and describe my father's behavior and
> I would look at my husband and he would be doing exactly
> the same thing. . . . So many times I was lonely for my
> husband with him sitting right there two feet from me.
> —RENATA

Renata's pain and shame in having replicated the very misery she swore to leave behind is not news to the countless children of alcoholics who grow up to marry other alcoholics, some more than once; to the many survivors of physical abuse who grow up to find themselves partnered with other abusers. *How can this be?* they all asked themselves as the terrible truth of what had happened dawned upon them: *How could I choose someone who would cause the very suffering I wanted to escape?* It's one thing to slip into something by mistake. But to enter into the selfsame horror while vowing all the while not to? How could I have done this?

The devil you know is better than the devil you don't know, I guess. Human beings have a powerful and unacknowledged conservative streak, a remarkable ability to home in on the familiar, for good or for ill, to recognize it under any number of disguises, and to capture it again for our very own. We also have a stunning capacity to deny the reality we see before us. We often think in one way but act in another, tell ourselves we are walking resolutely into our future when we are really searching frantically for a route into our own past. And we do this even if it was a past we hated when we lived there.

But does it have to be this way? Are we doomed to revisit our damaged earlier selves again and again? To live always and only in new versions of our families of origin, to build them anew everywhere we go? No, we are not doomed. We can do a new thing. Even if we have landed with a thump in the very prison we thought we had left behind, things need not be for us the way they've always been. But if things are to change, it can only be because we begin to do things differently. More of same just gets us more of same.

Renata *did* marry a man with the same disease her father had. It is hard not to think that some hidden sixth sense in her—one of which she was, and remains, unaware—chose him very carefully, and chose him for that reason. But there were other, better bonds between them than that sad historical one. After her initial denial, and after years of trying to cope with her old familiar sorrow in the old familiar way, she came to realize that she *could* choose another life. She could choose *not* to become her mother. The contrast between the two women's lives today is stark:

> My father has not received any help for depression ever. He is now eighty-five and is lying in bed twenty out of twenty-four hours. He has no friends, no interests, no hobbies; he has absolutely no life. He does not speak to my mother unless he has to. He hates the world. My mother will not leave his side.
>
> My husband, on the other hand, is slowly getting well again. After the last suicide attempt he has been prescribed Paxil and has been in therapy for over a year. I told him that I would not live with him if he did not get help.
>
> Now that I think of it, this is where we differ from my parents.
> —RENATA

Few things in life are harder than choosing against family tradition, whether that tradition is acknowledged (hard enough) or unacknowledged (even harder). Families do the things they do because they know of no other way to do them, and the training they give us in what life is about comes our way early, when we are most ready to absorb it indelibly. It is our first religion.

For many of us, that means idealizing our very ordinary parents, taking them as our household gods—for a while, anyway, until adolescence introduces us to the idea that they may not know everything there is to know about everything there is. We swim awkwardly in *that* sea of unwanted relativism for a while: if they are not oracles of absolute truth and perfect rectitude, do they have any magisterium left at all? If our parents don't know everything, can they really be said to know *anything*? We are not sure for a year or two, many of us, an uncertainty that usually lasts until we discover our own feet of clay, and then we begin the long process of learning to relate to our parents as human beings.

Growing up can be something else entirely for the children of the severely depressed.

> The day I got my menstrual period for the first time, I was in fourth grade. . . . My mother, who had been in a mental hospital for two months, had given me a brochure to read and told me to ask her if I had any questions. Luckily, I had read the brochure. . . . At the end of school on that day, I walked from school to the drugstore on Main Street.

I walked in and asked the pharmacist for a box of junior tampons. He blushed and told me to speak with Ann, his female assistant. She refused to sell me tampons, so I insisted that they call my father. He was embarrassed and told them to sell me anything I wanted. They finally agreed. I walked back home by myself (one mile) and practiced with a mirror until I got it right. I was nine years old. When my father returned home, he decided that things were OK, and he didn't have to deal with it. (His remedy for menstrual cramps, which I had, was a stiff shot of whiskey and several hours of sleep.)

I was alternately daughter, parent to my mother, homemaker for my father, and child of both parents—but never really a child, ever. . . . During all of this, neither of my parents recognized that I might need some counseling. My father told me that since the gene pool was so diverse, I would be just fine. . . .

One night, when I was sixteen, my mother woke me at 3 A.M. to tell me that there were Martians on the roof. She was wearing the clothes that I had laid out for my next day at school. She asked me not to wake my father but to come outside and watch the aliens landing on the roof. OK . . . So there we were, sitting on the curb in the dark, watching aliens on the roof. My father finally awoke at 6 A.M. and realized that we were not in the house. He saw us outside on the curb and called the first aid squad. He must have had some inkling that their services might be needed. I had no clue, except for the fact that I was outside, on the curb, with my mom, who was dressed in my clothes. The ambulance arrived, and my mother rushed into the house and locked herself in the bathroom. She would only let me in. I knocked on the door and identified myself, and she opened the door, I hit her with a tranquilizer injection that I had been trained to give her in just such an emergency. The squad came in, picked her up off the bathroom floor, strapped her onto a gurney, and took her directly to the state hospital. (I had practiced on oranges.) After they carried her out to the ambulance, I didn't get to see her for six weeks. I have never quite gotten over my role in this scenario. . . .

  After she left, I took a shower, ate breakfast, got dressed, and took the bus to school. I was a sophomore in high school.
    —LIZA

I can see her now: finding some other clothes to wear, since her mom had gone off in the ambulance in the outfit she had planned. Stepping out of the shower, wrapping her head in a towel. Gulping down her orange juice and making a piece of toast in the silent house, her father already gone. Running for the bus. Her smooth young face is without expression, her mouth a straight line onto which she applies lipstick. No tears.

  They are delicate, kids. You don't sit them down and say, *Now let's talk about your feelings.* They're still *afraid* of their feelings—Liza at sixteen, for instance: isn't an avalanche of feelings the very *last* thing she would want to start? Has she ever seen feelings lead anywhere that anybody sane would ever want to go? Feelings were what her mother had in such abundance, for heaven's sake, feelings that crippled and confused her and stole her away, feelings that turned her into her daughter's limping charge, rather than the wise guide and rock-solid support we all want our mothers to be. No, she would have said, how about let's *not* talk about my feelings? How about we *never* talk about them?

But she did, of course. Later on, when she grew up. She watched herself carefully when she became a mother, and so did her husband:

> From my very beginning . . . my mother could not recognize that she had even given birth to me, for nearly six months. Mine was a difficult and traumatic birth, and my mother just blotted the whole experience out of her memory. After those six months, in desperation, my father took pictures of me to the hospital, and she finally decided that she was indeed my mother. . . .
>
> Years later, when R. and I had our own children, my parents and husband watched to see if I would have the same issues. . . . Thankfully, I bonded with both babies at birth, and things were fine for many years.
>
> —LIZA

Liza did not escape severe depression, although she was never as cripplingly ill as her mother had been. Liza lives in a different age: better medicines, better therapy. She has a more open attitude toward mental illness. With years of therapy and medication behind her and still firmly in place, her life is very different from the extended heartbreak that was her mother's. And there is no doubt that surviving her terrible early experiences strengthened her. They don't always, of course: some people emerge permanently stunted from the same things that galvanize other people. It's not always easy to understand why some survive and thrive and some do not. But even the survivors and thrivers, like Liza, bear the scars.

I have spoken to many survivors of severe family affliction—its legacy is often terrible and deep, and it is usually obvious. But there is another more paradoxical affliction: sometimes the very fact of success and prosperity in the life of someone who has not done the spadework of deepening the spirit so that it rests solidly on the rock of a reasonable balance between the inner life and the outer world can create a "but what have you done lately?" context for living. Someone else is always richer, faster, smarter, thinner, or more successful—no matter what you've done, it isn't enough. Sometimes this comes directly from a high-powered family's inability to understand and accommodate a more soulful child. And sometimes it just comes with the culture of modern life, which insists on our chronic thirst for more and more as a condition of being part of it. It takes guts and a climate of moral support to refuse its demands.

But families have some power over the devastating effects of an uncritical embrace of a competitive and often cruel world. Who are you, really? Are you what you *have?* What you *do?* What you *know?* I look at the latest photographs of our newest grandchild, sent through the Internet from an ocean away. He is not yet a week old. He knows next to nothing and cannot survive on his own. He is a person of no power. And yet I cannot take my eyes off that little face in those pictures. I would give my life for his in a heartbeat. He has done nothing to earn this devotion but be born into this world. That's it.

This is the key: the fact of our being is sufficient cause for God's celebration. We need look no further for validation. We are children of God, put here to delight in the world for as long as we are privileged to be here. Yes, we have projects and duties, goals and ambitions, but none of them can make or break us. The sufficiency of my little grandson's face in my eyes is complete, and that is just the way God sees all of us.

So it is love that trains us best to withstand the world's wrongheaded pressures. When someone looks at us in that way, we begin to know what it is to be surrounded by love, no matter what else happens to us in life. "What else" can encompass a lot: not all of it will be joyful and some of it will be terrible. Some of it will be internal and chemical; some will arise from outside us. We cannot prevent all of it. I hope that this book, and the experiences of the people in it, have made that clear.

But we can resolve to live together in a way that does not make it worse. We can reach out for help when we need it, and we can tell the truth about those moments. We can understand slick promises of a world in which there is no such thing as defeat as the lies they are.

And we can acknowledge that this life is not all there is: we have a context, and it is not just historical and not just physical. It is also eternal.

NOTES

Prologue

1. Eloise Blanchard, "By the Waters of Babylon," unpublished poem. Used with permission.

Chapter 2: A Learning Experience

1. Julian of Norwich, *Showings*, ed. E. Colledge, J. Walsh, and J. LeClerq (Mahwah, N.J.: Paulist Press, 1977), p. 205.

2. Ibid., p. 207.

3. Henry Langhorne, "Worry," *As Fate Would Have It: New Poems* (Pensacola, Fla.: Pelican Press, 2007), p. 38.

Chapter 3: I Just Don't Feel Anything

1. Charles Colwell, *Collision of Worlds: A Priest's Life* (New York: iUniverse, 2008), p. 30.

2. Ibid., p. 31.

3. Gerald May, *The Dark Night of the Soul* (San Francisco: HarperOne, 2005), p. 158.

Chapter 5: Charged with the Care of Souls

1. George Herbert, "Aaron," in *The Complete English Poems*, ed. J. Tobin (Harmondsworth, England: Penguin, 1991), p. 164.

Chapter 7: This Is My Last Hope

1. Sam Gardiner, "Electric Poem," *The North*, 2005, 36. Retrieved Nov. 22, 2008, from http://www.poetrymagazines. org.uk/magazine/record.asp?id=15289.

Chapter 8: Sorrowful Mysteries

1. Christopher Hitchens, "Teresa, Bright and Dark," *Newsweek Web Exclusive*, Aug. 29, 2007. Retrieved Nov. 22, 2008, from http://www.newsweek.com/id/38603.

2. Mother Teresa, *Come Be My Light: The Private Writings of the "Saint of Calcutta,"* ed. B. Kolodiejchuck (New York: Doubleday, 2007), pp. 149, 165.

3. Ibid., p. 40.

4. Ibid., p. 44.

5. Ibid., p. 113.

6. Ibid., p. 163.

7. Ibid., p. 230.

8. Christopher Hitchens, in David Von Biema, "Mother Teresa's Crisis of Faith," *Time*, Aug. 23, 2007, p. 1.

9. Mother Teresa, *Come Be My Light*, p. 219.

10. Ibid., p. 306.

11. Ibid., pp. 5, 152.

12. Ibid., p. 164.

13. Ibid., p. 214.

Chapter 9: The Dark Night

1. Saint John of the Cross, *The Collected Works of St. John of the Cross*, trans. Kieran Kavanaugh and Otilio Rodriguez [electronic version] (Washington, D.C.: Institute of Carmelite Studies, 1991).

2. Saint Teresa of Avila, *The Collected Works of St. Teresa of Avila*, trans. Kieran Kavanaugh and Otilio Rodriguez [electronic version] (Washington, D.C.: Institute of Carmelite Studies, 1985).

3. Dante Alighieri, *Inferno*, canto I.

Chapter 11: Wanting to Die

1. William Shakespeare, *Hamlet*, act 3, scene 1.

FURTHER READING

Moody, Rick. *The Black Veil: A Memoir with Digressions*. New York: Little, Brown, 2002.

Palmer, Parker. *Let Your Life Speak. Listening for the Voice of Vocation*. San Francisco: Jossey-Bass, 2000.

Solomon, Andrew. *The Noonday Demon: An Atlas of Depression*. New York: Scribner, 2001.

Styron, William. *Darkness Visible*. New York: Vintage, 1990.

THE AUTHOR

Barbara Cawthorne Crafton is an Episcopal priest and author. She heads The Geranium Farm, an institute for the promotion of spiritual growth. The Farm publishes her Almost-Daily eMo, a meditation read online by tens of thousands worldwide at http://www.geraniumfarm.org. She has served a number of churches, including historic Trinity Church, Wall Street, Saint John's-in-the-Village in Greenwich Village, and Saint Clement's in Manhattan's theater district. She was a maritime chaplain on the New York waterfront and served as a chaplain at Ground Zero after the attacks on the World Trade Center. She currently serves Saint James, the American church in Florence, Italy. A spiritual director, Crafton leads retreats and teaches throughout the United States and abroad. An actor and director, she has produced or directed many plays in New York and elsewhere and for many years has combined the lively arts with the life of faith. She is seen frequently on the Hallmark television network and has been profiled extensively in the electronic and print media. Her radio scripts and articles have won prizes that include the coveted

Gabriel Award in religious broadcasting and numerous Polly Bond Awards from Episcopal Communicators.

Her many books include books of essays (*The Sewing Room, Yes! We'll Gather at the River, Some Things You Just Have to Live With*), books of daily meditations (*Let Us Bless the Lord* (Volumes 1–4), *Meditations on the Psalms, Finding Time for Serenity,* and several others), a book of poetry (*Blessed Paradoxes*), and a book about the current wars in Iraq and Afghanistan in the aftermath of the World Trade Center bombing (*Mass in Time of War*).

She is married to Richard Quaintance, an English professor.

LET YOUR LIFE SPEAK

Listening for the Voice of Vocation

Parker J. Palmer

ISBN 978-0-7879-4735-4
Hardcover | 128 pp.

Discover your path in life

Let Your Life Speak is an insightful and moving meditation on finding one's true calling. The book's title is a time-honored Quaker admonition, usually taken to mean "Let the highest truths and values guide everything you do." But Palmer reinterprets those words, drawing on his own search for selfhood. "Before you tell your life what you intend to do with it," he writes, "listen for what it intends to do with you. Before you tell your life what truths and values you have decided to live up to, let your life tell you what truths you embody, what values you represent." Sharing stories of frailty and strength, of darkness and light, Palmer will show you that vocation is not a goal to be achieved but a gift to be received.

Parker J. Palmer is a highly respected writer, teacher, and activist. Author of seven books, including such widely praised books as *The Courage to Teach*, *The Promise of Paradox*, and *A Hidden Wholeness,* he holds a Ph.D. from the University of California at Berkeley. He is a member of the Religious Society of Friends (Quaker) and lives in Madison, Wisconsin.

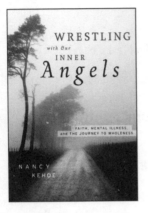

WRESTLING WITH OUR INNER ANGELS

Faith, Mental Illness, and the
Journey to Wholeness

Nancy Kehoe

ISBN 978-0-470-45541-8
Hardcover | 192 pp.

WRESTLING WITH OUR INNER ANGELS is Nancy Kehoe's compelling, intimate, and moving story of how she brought her background as a psychologist and a nun in the Religious of the Sacred Heart to bear in the groups she formed to explore the role of faith and spirituality in the treatment and lives of patients with mental illness. Through fascinating stories of her own spiritual journey, she gives readers of all backgrounds and interests new insights into the inner lives of the mentally ill and new ways of thinking about the role of spirituality and faith in all our lives.

Nancy Kehoe is a nun (Religious of the Sacred Heart) and distinguished clinician known for her pioneering work with the mentally ill, with more than 25 years of experience incorporating religious belief and its role in treatment. She is a Clinical Instructor in Psychology in the Department of Psychiatry at the Cambridge Health Alliance, affiliated with Harvard Medical School. Through her website **www.expandingconnections.com**, she makes herself available as a speaker, consultant, and trainer, to both religious and health care organizations.

Available May 2009

A HIDDEN WHOLENESS

The Journey Toward an Undivided Life

Parker J. Palmer

ISBN 978-0-470-45376-6
Paperback | 150 pp.

"This book is a treasure—an inspiring, useful blueprint for building safe places where people can commit to 'act in every situation in ways that honor the soul.'" —**Publishers Weekly**

In *A Hidden Wholeness*, Parker J. Palmer reveals the same compassionate intelligence and informed heart that shaped his best-selling books, *Let Your Life Speak* and *The Courage to Teach.* Here he speaks to our yearning to live undivided lives in a world filled with the forces of fragmentation. *A Hidden Wholeness* weaves together four themes: the shape of an integral life, the meaning of community, teaching and learning for transformation, and nonviolent social change.

Defining a "circle of trust" as "a space between us that honors the soul," Palmer shows how people in settings ranging from friendship to organizational life can support each other on the journey toward living "divided no more." The hundreds of thousands of people who know Parker J. Palmer's books will be glad to find the journey continued here–and readers new to his work will be glad they joined that journey.

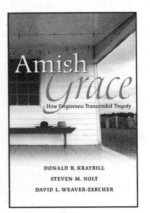

AMISH GRACE

How Forgiveness Transcended Tragedy

Donald B. Kraybill, Steven M. Nolt,
David L. Weaver-Zercher

ISBN 978-0-7879-9761-8
Hardcover | 221 pp.

"A casebook on forgiveness valuable for ALL Christians. It drills beneath the theory to their practice and even deeper to the instructions of Jesus." —**Dr. Julia Upton,** provost, St. John's University

The remarkable response of the Amish community to the horrific shooting of ten schoolgirls at Nickel Mines, Pennsylvania, in October 2006 stunned the larger world. *Amish Grace* tells the incredible story of this community's reaction to the senseless shooting and explores its profoundly countercultural practice of forgiveness.

Amish Grace explores the many questions the Nickel Mines incident raises about the religious beliefs that led the Amish to forgive so quickly. In a world where religion spawns so much violence and vengeance, the surprising act of Amish forgiveness begs for deeper consideration.